The Mighty Man Manual Participant Workbook

Edition II

By Jon Snyder

www.MightyManManual.com

info@MightyManManual.com

The Mighty Man Manual Participant Workbook
Edition II
©2014 by Jon Snyder. All rights reserved.

ISBN-13: 9781491065938
ISBN-10: 1491065931

www.MightyManManual.com
info@MightyManManual.com

Excerpts from the Mighty Man Manual © 2009, Mighty Man Manual Edition II © 2014 by Jon Snyder. All rights reserved. Published by Jon Snyder and Theos Publishing, P.O. Box 314, Edgemont, PA 19028.

Unless otherwise noted, Scripture quotations are taken from the New King James Version, © 1979, 1980, 1982, 1984 by Thomas Nelson, Inc. All right reserved.

CONTENTS

Introduction to the Mighty Man Manual Workbook Series

Welcome dear reader. You are about to embark on a life-changing 8 weeks! The Bible says, *"Eye has not seen, nor ear heard, Nor have entered into the heart of man The things which God has prepared for those who love Him"* (1 Cor. 2:9). Your desire to be free from lust in any form, whether it be pornography or sexual addiction reflects that God is already at work in your heart to give you the desire to love Him more and honor Him with your mind and body! So even before you start to read, know that God IS at work in you, that you have taken your first steps toward freedom and be confident that *"He who has begun a good work in you will complete it until the day of Jesus Christ"* (Php. 1:6).

Over the next eight weeks, you will learn more of the depth of God's love for you and experience the divine empowering of His grace in your life to overcome and become more than a conqueror in Christ. But most importantly, you will see the foundations laid for lasting personal transformation in your heart.

This workbook series is designed to give you a plan of action that will take you or your men's group through an introductory week plus 7 subsequent weeks (8 weeks total) of teaching that take the primary benchmark themes contained in *The Mighty Man Manual* to a much deeper level. These next weeks are potentially the most important time you will ever spend in pursuit of total inner healing and deliverance from sinful addictions. This time is purposefully designed to act as an intense period of heart cleansing in Christ.

Utilizing the MMM Workbook
for independent study

This workbook can be used by individuals or as part of a small fellowship group. Each week's lessons can be used to go deeper into the teaching of the Mighty Man Manual. However, know that along the way you will continue to face temptations and struggles. For this reason, we stress the importance of having support. *"Two are better than one, Because they have a good reward for their labor. For if they fall, one will lift up his companion. But woe to him who is alone when he falls, For he has no one to help him up"* (Ec. 4:9,10). You may not have a designated small group going through this with you, but we encourage you to find a fellowship and prayer partner who can be there for encouragement, accountability and most importantly, prayer covering and support.

Whereas the goal of this book is to bring about real heart change, know that this won't happen overnight and you may be truly blessed by the encouragement, and added benefits of not "going it alone." Your support person may be a close friend, a spouse or a member of a small group at your church. This format with support allows you to enjoy the weekly, intentional prayer covering and accountability you would receive if participating in a group setting. However, for the reader who doesn't have a convenient prayer partner, we trust that God who called you to this time of deliverance is able to make all grace abound to you and fully supply all your needs for this time.

Utilizing the MMM Workbook
for small group format.

Churches, men's groups and counseling ministries may request an Official Teacher's Guide that will supplement this workbook for use by group moderators. the MMM Small Group Teacher's Guide will show you how to organize the group into prayer and accountability teams, moderate and teach each week, facilitate group interaction and sharing and more. If your church or other small group wishes to utilize this program, please make sure to obtain a copy of the Teacher's Guide from Mighty Man Ministries to facilitate your weekly sessions.

With the exception of the Introductory Session, each Session is designed to fill 1-1.5 hours of small group format as follows.

Brief Weekly Introduction – 1-5 minutes
We recommend always opening with prayer followed by a short opening.

Object Lesson – 5-10 minutes
The object lesson is designed to be interactive, thought provoking and give men something that they will remember in a different way than they would a didactic teaching or reading.

Didactic Teaching or Group Discussion – 15-20 minutes
Many small group leaders like to open their groups with a time of teaching or with moderated sharing and discussion of key points that God has been revealing over the week. While there will be likely teaching spread throughout the group discussion of the Workbook questions, this time can help present ideas and a learning environment that is different from the more structured question-by-question Workbook Q&A. We recommend that this be limited to 15-20 minutes to allow time for facilitated group interaction and learning followed by prayer time.

Facilitated Discussion of Workbook Questions – 30 minutes
The teacher should hand out workbook materials with enough lead time for men to thoughtfully go through the materials, take any self-examination quizzes, answer questions and meditate on the scriptures

provided. These various exercises will become the backbone of the discussion each following week and should lead into group prayer time.

Prayer – 20-30 minutes

All real heart change comes from the Lord. Therefore the MMM and its Workbook emphasize prayer both individually and corporately. The Workbook presents a number of different prayer topics following each session. Teachers are encouraged to seek the Lord in how He may want to augment that individual prayer in the group setting. Often individuals who have experienced particular breakthroughs in any given week may want to pray and minister to others. Accountability groups may be utilized to facilitate individual one-on-one prayer needs as well as minister to one another throughout the week.

Introductory Session
to the Mighty Man Manual

OPENING PRAYER:

Father, You are the potter I am Your clay. I give you my mind, heart and body to mold. Grant me the grace right now to hear only Your truth and to be transformed. In Jesus' name, amen.

GOING DEEPER:
ADDITIONAL TEACHING FOR DEEPER UNDERSTANDING

Any runner will tell you, the first fifteen minutes of their workouts are the most difficult. In the early stages of an athlete's training session, the circulatory system is still at rest; the muscles aren't warmed up; the cellular and lymphatic channels aren't evacuating metabolic waste at the level they need to be during high endurance activity; even the athlete's mind is still in "rest mode." They call this grueling early stage "the Runner's Hump."

Every athlete must train themselves to anticipate the runner's hump and set their mind and heart on the finish line and not allow the pain of getting the proverbial 10-ton ball of momentum rolling to stop them. You are about to embark on a unique time of RE-TRAINING. You will be re-learning how to respond to temptations; re-learning how to cope with your own areas of weakness; learning how to relate to God in new ways; learning how to love yourself and trust God's love for you on a whole new level; you will even be learning how to live life with a void where you once had lust to fill your time and thoughts. **There will be a "runner's hump" to get over.**

The first four or five weeks will be the hardest. Studies have shown that the chemical and hormonal physical response to pornography can be as habit forming as heroin addiction. Furthermore there are soul ties that happen as we are exposed to pornography that take time to abate. These factors make it so critical that we do everything in our power to leave no room for slip ups as we start out for life and heart change. This is your proverbial hump to get over. This first week's session is not so much to teach you new things... that will come in due time. Rather this first week is to set your mind in agreement with what you are about to undertake and set up your circumstances accordingly. Paul says: *Do you not know that those who run in a race all run, but one receives the prize? Run in such a way that you may obtain it. Therefore I run thus: not with uncertainty. Thus I fight: not as one who beats the air. But I discipline my body and bring it into subjection, lest, when I have preached to others, I myself should become disqualified* (1 Cor. 9:24, 26, 27).

Know that you will be tested. Know that the first few weeks may be the most difficult thing you ever have to do. But also know that it will be worth it and that it WILL get easier. Know that the things that you "give up" are nothing in comparison to the riches of knowing the Lord more deeply and walking in your calling. With that in mind, keep your eyes on the prize and enter into this time of training with the resolve to become the Mighty Man that God will bring forth.

MIGHTY MEN ASSEMBLE:

Don't be discouraged by the fact that this won't be easy. Rather, let that fact stir up something primal and powerful in your heart. Most of us know gentle Jesus, meek and mild. Let us stir up the revelation of the Lord of Hosts (translated as the God of armies). Revelation tells us that when Christ returns, it is with a sword, a robe drenched in blood and we, at His side, will slay every enemy on the last day. There is a warrior in each one of us. It is time for the warrior to awake. What's the alternative? How long are you content for lust to rule over you and steal your blessings? It is time, mighty man of God to rise up and do what you were born again to do: destroy the works of the devil, crush satan's head under your heel and take your place as a full heir and son of God.

Freedom is possible. Freedom is now! Don't just "try" to get free as you go through this book. Rather, get free! The truth is that you are already a new creation in Christ. You already have His Spirit in you. You have a new nature. But the devil has done a great job causing you to identify with the old man and make you live as the image of fallen man rather than as the person he fears, a mighty man created in the image of the Lord of Hosts. It is time to lay hold violently of the freedom that has been purchased for you; for "the Kingdom of Heaven suffers violence, and the violent take it by force (Mt. 11:12).

There are some things in the Kingdom that come through rest and there are some that come by war. This is the latter. If you dare to go through this book, prepare yourself like a soldier going to war. "Those who run in a race all run, but one receives the prize - Run in such a way that you may obtain it (1 Co. 9:24)." 2 Corinthians 7:11 tells us what Godly repentance looks like, "What diligence it produced in you, what clearing of yourselves, what indignation, what fear, what vehement desire, what zeal, what vindication! In all things you proved yourselves to be clear in this matter." There is no such thing as half-hearted Biblical repentance. If your repentance doesn't have zeal, vehement desire and vindication in it, you haven't repented of your sin yet.

Failure is not an option. If you are in Christ, victory is your destiny. Anything less is meaningless and passing. If you are in Christ, your heart burns for this freedom. Allow the Holy Spirit to kindle this in you if you are not burning with conviction already. Channel that zeal into the pursuit of God (because it is His Spirit in you that will achieve the victory, not your zeal, which waxes and wanes). Nothing that you truly want is in that old, dead life. There is NOTHING you can ever see or do in that old life that you haven't already. It will never fill the needs in your heart. In *The Matrix*, Neo is about to allow his fears drive him back to his old "comfortable" life when Trinity grabs him by the arm and reminds him, "You have been down that road... you know *exactly* where it leads." Settle it now. The life of faith is scary, but is what your heart really needs. The life of sin has a form of comfort... but it isn't what your soul is designed for. It is nothing but the slow, painful death of the part of you that is really alive.

Are you ready to take up your sword, shield and armor of faith? Settle the following in your heart and say these things out loud:
-    I want to be a mighty man for the Lord in my generation.
-    Christ purchased my freedom; I am free; my life is going to show it now.
-    Lust and pornography has nothing that I truly want.

9

- When the devil pushes his temptation in my face and loins, I am going to destroy him mercilessly by the grace and power of the Spirit in me.
- I will do whatever it takes to dedicate myself to the Lord and this teaching over the next 8 weeks.
- I will do whatever it takes to eradicate every avenue and opportunity for lust in my circumstances, heart and home.
- A new life starts now.

PRACTICAL ADVICE:

Everyone has weakness and weak moments. Don't think that because you feel strong in this moment, these feelings will last for the rest of your life. The devil knows how to "read us" and exploit us at the opportune time. For this reason we strongly encourage participants to take an honest look at some of the options that will be a deterrent to moments of weakness. The group setting is able to provide some of these benefits. If you are going through this individually, think about how you may work these into your freedom plan.

Prayer Covering: Do make sure that you have people praying for you daily in this time. Utilize your prayer support and even call them when you are struggling. If you aren't part of a group, if possible, ask a friend, spouse, pastor or trusted mentor to pray for you daily.

Accountability: While getting through the initial, difficult season, knowing that you will have to give an honest, daily account can be an added motivator to fight harder. There will be a time when you won't need daily accountability, but take advantage of this help now.

External Solutions: If you are able, seriously consider doing without a computer during this time. Or if your family uses a central computer, have your spouse put a password on it for you and use it only during family times. Many smart phones also have the ability to turn off web browsing or put browsing under password protection. Think about EVERY possible way that you can gratify lust and take every measure to safeguard these. Again, failure is not an option. You MUST make today the day of freedom or it will be NEVER.

If you must use a computer or devices on which you can find pornography during this time, consider third party software to monitor your internet use. You can even place software on your computer that will email your accountability partner a list of every website you visit.

The goal isn't to live with ongoing accountability and a lock-and-key on your computer. The goal is to achieve real heart change. If that doesn't take place and your heart is still searching for sin, you'll find it eventually. But heart change takes time and if you have a serious addiction with weekly or daily slips, the addiction to lust not only has spiritual and mental draw but actually has been proven to elicit a chemical response in the brain with additional physiological addiction formation. Lust addictions can be every bit as difficult to break as any substance abuse and there will be an intense battle that may require more than just willpower - and only you know your limits and weaknesses. This IS your time of freedom. In these initial weeks or months, you may need to get drastic if you want drastic results. Be confident that every day the Holy Spirit will strengthen your inner man and bring you into freedom; but every soldier must go into battle with a knowledge of his arsenal of weapons and how that arsenal will help cover any chinks in their armor.

COVENANT PLEDGE

Go into this with more than just an unspoken idea. Put your resolve in writing. A written covenant is a powerful tool. The following page will present some statements of commitment, a Covenant Document, to declare your resolve and commitment for the pursuit of freedom to you and your group. Take personal ownership of the following statements and take this as a promise to yourself to really go after your freedom with all your heart. Take these next statements and make a covenant with yourself, your fellow participants in this workbook and with God.

1. I hereby commit myself to the Lord, to my family, to my Christian brothers and to this teaching for these next 8 weeks.
2. I will be honest and accurate with my accountability partner. I will not add the sin of lying to the sin of lust if I have stumbled.
3. I will, with all my heart, all my soul and all my strength love the Lord My God, keep His word and fight for my Freedom in Christ with everything that is in me during this time.
4. I will make the time in my life and schedule to read the lessons and spend time with the Lord every day so that He may cause them to go deep in my heart.
5. I will pray daily for the brothers entrusted to my covering. I will go to war with the enemy for them as often as they need me to. I will fight for my brothers' freedom by keeping myself pure.
6. I will wake up each morning and rededicate myself to this commitment, no matter what my feelings may otherwise dictate.
7. I hereby set my name to this covenant that I may be faithful to God and my brothers.

Signature(s):

CUTTING LUST FROM YOUR LIFE

You are about to embark on a life-changing journey that will both remove lust from your life and at the same time open your eyes to the fruitfulness of life as God intended it to be as you walk with Him more and more deeply and in your calling. There is no comparison between what you will give up and what you will get; but don't think that the enemy will let this stronghold go without a fight. For many, this will be one of the hardest things that you will ever have to do. These instructions may seem extreme to some, but for many there is no other solution than to take extreme measures. Fasting is a Biblical principle that also seems extreme; we encourage you to look at this as your 40 day "fast" from lust.

EXERCISE: CLEANING HOUSE

Let me get real for a moment. You can't say, "I want pornography out of my life." or "I want sexual addiction out of my life." and leave open doors for lust in other areas. Lust is lust. You can't have some lust in one area and think that it won't infect your whole being. We must break all agreements with ALL forms of lust if we are to get free. Some of you reading this may have already done the following to "clean house." For others, this step will require some heavy sacrifice and the removal of old, familiar habits as well as personal possessions that incite lust. Jesus said it this way, *"And if your eye causes you to sin, pluck it out and cast it from you. It is better for you to enter into life with one eye, rather than having two eyes, to be cast into hell fire* (Mt. 18:9)." Cutting sin out of your life requires determination and removing things that can cause you to sin.

SELF CHECKLIST:

Do you posses anything that will give the enemy space in your home or your heart? Use this checklist and turn your home into a place that is a "lust-free-zone."

☐ **Get rid of "the collection"**

This should be self-apparent: you can't plan to get pornography out of your life and have a "stash" of pornography. If you have anything saved on your computer or any magazines or movies, now is the time to destroy the stash. This may need to be done with your accountability group for moral support especially if you have had this pornography for a long time. The power and emotional soul ties with your first magazine or movie can be so strong for some men that it is every bit as difficult as breaking up with a girlfriend. If this is the case, get creative with your group. Plan a camp out and burn the collections in a fire. This can be symbolic for the men (just make sure to have everyone turn their back on the fire when the box goes up so that any printed images aren't exposed to the group if you do something like this). Clear your internet history and make sure any places you have saved files have been deleted and the recycle bin emptied.

☐ **Get hard on the soft stuff**

Now let's get even more serious. Do you have any Hollywood movies (not porn) that have sex scenes with nudity in them; or that are particularly fueled with lust? Are there any movies with racy scenes that "don't show anything" but are particularly sensual? Do you have any comedies that are particularly immoral or treat lust and sex with levity? I'm sorry to say, these movies should also be thrown out. Whether you put an "R" label or an "X" label on entertainment depicting lustful scenarios, your soul will be stirred with lust and your mind will form agreements with these strongholds. Lust is lust. Many of today's "acceptable" movies would have been seen as pornographic or lewd in the past and should be viewed as Christ would view them.

Romans 1:32 teaches that if we know the righteous judgments of God and approve of people who violate them, we are guilty of the same sin as the people practicing the act. We need to get serious about lust. You can't say, "I want lust out of my life." But allow movies with lust and sex in the home. This is hypocritical and creates space for lust in our hearts.

We must look at all of our movies and ask if we would sit down and watch them with Jesus. If not, why would we watch that on our own? Look at your movie collection and determine if you would let your son or daughter watch that movie (every scene). If you wouldn't, remember that God wants us to come to the Kingdom "as a little child."

☐ Clean Sweep

Use the above advice and apply it to all areas of your life and all of your possessions. Do you have any magazines that the world wouldn't classify as pornography but that have pictorials with partially clothed women? These are filled with lust. Are there video games that are particularly lustful? Do you have art, drawings, etc? Pray about this and ask God if there is anything in your possession that you would be ashamed of in His presence.

☐ Purity

Pre-marital sex or fornication is also running rampant in Christianity. Men, let us get sober and serious about the Word of God for a moment. The Bible clearly states that NO fornicator, no person having sex outside of marriage will enter the Kingdom of God or have an inheritance with God (Eph. 5:5, 1 Cor. 6:9-10, Gal. 5:19, Col. 3:5,etc.). You can't get lust out in one area and be practicing lust in other areas. Eradicating one type of lust from your life while inviting another form in is like trying to bail water out of the tub with the faucet running.

This is a serious issue and I need to bring it up because I love you and want God's best for your life. There are two types of believers struggling in this area of fornication: the immature believer who keeps messing up (but who truly wants purity in their relationship) and the rebellious person who doesn't want purity or to surrender this area to God. Rebellion and immaturity are completely different. For the person fooling around outside of marriage without the intention to give it up, this is more serious than simply getting lust out of your life. The Bible teaches that one comes to **repentance** when they are saved. How then can one be saved if there is a glaring area of **unrepentant** sin and an **unwillingness** to forsake it and repent of it? For the believer who wants freedom, there is all the grace in the world. For the individual who is hard-hearted toward God, I implore that you surrender to Him. Otherwise, give up the pseudo-Christian charade and do not be fooled into believing that you are saved. Grace is not a license to sin. Grace is the power to stop sinning.

Many single men may ask, "Where is 'the line?'" or "How far can I go with my girlfriend?" That is like asking the question, "How close to fire can I get before I get burned?" We shouldn't have the attitude of how close we can get to sin when we are called to flee from lust. Why not ask the question, "How pure can I get?" However, to give a more practical answer, as a general rule, any activity that gets a young couple "turned on" is most likely past "the line." Arousal and lust often go hand-in-hand. For this reason, fooling around before marriage trains our souls to think that arousal, sexual excitement and lust are the same thing. This is why so many people falsely believe that "sex is better" outside of marriage. What they are experiencing is the fact that the demonic frenzy of lust has been removed from the equation once they are married. Christian men must understand that there is no lust in marriage; and we do ourselves a disservice training our souls in premarital lust and thinking that sex in marriage will feel the same. This activity damages your marital sex life before it even begins. Brethren, cut all lust, fooling around, fornication, adultery and fantasy from your life.

☐ Keeping your marriage bed holy

Lust in marriage is not just limited to adultery (though adultery is an obvious activity that should be stopped immediately). Married men are also encouraged to stop anything with their wives that entices them to lust. For example, if you have had a particular fetish in pornography, it is almost impossible for you to practice that act with your wife without opening your soul up to familiar lusts again. Simply put, you can't have logged hundreds of hours associating one type of sex act with lust and "turn those feelings off" when doing it in the bedroom. Similarly, fantasizing about another woman during sex or role play that pretends your wife is another woman is another obvious invitation to lust. We live in a society that has forgotten that sex is a Holy Sacrament and we have perverted it to a pastime.

Lust steals and uses our spouse for our own gains. Marital intimacy should have love at its core. As the love in the bedroom increases, the pleasure also goes deeper. Holy sex should be wonderful, passionate, gratifying and exciting; it should "fill your love tank" because both parties are giving love. Lustful lovemaking can never make love. Therefore, millions of men go through their marriage with a hole in their heart wondering why they aren't satisfied and falsely believing that there is something wrong with their wives.

One other point that should be mentioned: if you have pictures, videos, poems or other keepsakes of your wife that are linked to pre-marital sex that you may have had with her, you may have to make a hard decision and part with them.

WORKBOOK MATERIALS

Reflect and answer the following questions from this week's study.

1) Think about Jon's story. Do you see any areas in your own life where this sin has escalated in frequency or in the type of things that you watch?

_____

_____

2) How important is it to get lust out of your life before it gets worse?

_____

_____

_____

3) One of the pivotal moments of victory comes in first believing that you can be free. That is the birthing point of faith. Do you believe that you can be free from this sin? How will that attitude change what you do, how you live and how you respond to temptation?

_____

_____

_____

_____

_____

4) Are you struggling to act on any of the actions in the self-checklist or other teachings from this week's reading or workbook? Do you need to get the advice and help of someone you trust to help work through this issue?

_____

_____

PRAYER

Sample prayer of dedication to purity:

Lord Jesus, you gave up everything for me. You took all my sins. You took all my shame. You purchased me back from the grip of the enemy. You gave me a new identity and salvation. I thank you. I desire that You should receive the reward for Your sacrifice; that I should have no other gods before You; that I should love You with all my heart, all my soul, all my mind and all my strength. This is my desire. Please fill me with Your Spirit that I shouldn't walk in the desires of my flesh. Please birth true repentance in my heart as well as the power to believe that I can be free from this sin. I dedicate myself to You now and ask you for the grace of salvation to come to this area of my life now also.

Week 1:
Grace

MIGHTY MAN MANUAL READING:

Chapter 4 - More than You can Bear – unlocking the
power of grace

OPENING PRAYER:

Father, You are the potter I am Your clay. I give you my mind, heart and body to mold. Grant me the grace right now to hear only Your truth and to be transformed. In Jesus' name, amen.

Going Deeper:
Additional Teaching for Deeper Understanding

"If YOU are disappointed in YOU when YOU mess up it was YOUR strength you were relying on." This is a cornerstone principle as we lay a foundation that is free from shame, empowered by love and full of grace.

DEVELOPING A FULL, BIBLICAL UNDERSTANDING OF GRACE WILL BE ONE OF THE MOST LIFE-CHANGING REVELATIONS YOU WILL EVER ENCOUNTER! A pastor who wrote our ministry summed up the importance of this session best, "I've personally taught dozens of sermons on grace, heard *hundreds* of sermons on it from every angle and just realized I never really understood it until I read the Mighty Man Manual." Grace is possibly one of the most under-taught, yet most essential topics in all of Christianity. Most Christians understand one aspect of it: that we are saved by grace through faith (Eph. 2:8). This, however, is only the very foundations of the full understanding of grace: that the mercy and forgiveness of God comes to undeserving sinners through grace; and that we, being completely incapable of earning or attaining salvation or forgiveness on our own merit, receive access to such a miracle through the empowering of grace at the time of salvation. But this is just the tip of the iceberg. First grace saves our lives... then grace changes our lives. There is very little teaching on the other Biblical functions of grace past its role in salvation. Do you know that the Bible teaches that literally EVERYTHING that is imparted to the believer comes through grace also?

Strong's Bible Dictionary calls grace, "the divine influence upon the heart, and its reflection in the life." Notice that definition is much broader than a simple statement about forgiveness, etc. What it is saying is that grace is the impartation of heavenly power and influence upon the undeserving human recipient in a way that tangibly and

21

meaningfully manifests in life. Think about what we really mean when we say someone is "graceful." That common use of the term indicates that rather than oafish, clumsy movement, it is as though the person exhibiting "grace" upon their movement is moving in a "divinely" beautiful manner. This idea of heavenly force operating in, on and through a person can help us understand the larger view of grace and how it can radically impact our ability to walk in victory in every area of life. When we access grace in any area of life we move into a heavenly-empowered dynamic and even our fight against sins becomes less clunky, less self-empowered and more gracefully Christ-powered.

Grace is bigger than just forgiveness of sins. Luke 2:40 tells us that Jesus needed grace for His earthly ministry; but we know it could not have been related to forgiveness of sins. We must learn to access the function of grace that was essential for Jesus as fully man to access the divine power that gives God's empowerment to earthly vessels. ALL the blessings of heaven and all of God's manifest ability in you comes by and through grace. Just as grace gives us access to God's forgiveness and salvation, grace is also the means by which our lives, hearts, thoughts and circumstances are ongoingly transformed by the power of God! I often liken grace to an astronaut on a spacewalk. He is connected to the space shuttle by a tube and is protected by bubble we call a spacesuit. This bubble and hose convey and surround him with life-giving essentials like oxygen in an otherwise hostile environment that would kill him instantly. This is like grace: we are surrounded and protected by God's sovereign will from hostile forces that we can't even contemplate 24/7; and every good and perfect, heavenly force comes to us by grace. Grace is our heavenly lifeline in this earthly walk.

Look at how many things the Bible says come by grace (and this is only a partial list!):
- Romans 4:16 – the promises of Abraham all come by grace
- Romans 11:5 – election to your heavenly call comes by grace
- Romans 12:6, 1 Peter 4:10 – gifts of the Spirit according to our
- MEASURE of grace (there are different measures of grace)

- Romans 15:15 – boldness
- 2 Corinthians 9:8 – all grace for all sufficiency in all things, an
- abundance for every good work
- 2 Corinthians 12:9 – sufficiency despite our own sins and weaknesses
- Ephesians 4:7 – individual measure of Christ's gift
- 2 Timothy 1:9 – our holy calling
- 2 Timothy 2:1 – strength
- Titus 2:11 – salvation
- Hebrews 4:16 – mercy and help in time of need
- James 4:6 – power to resist the enemy

ALL these things come by GRACE! Grace affects every area of our lives and everything that we receive from God because we are sinners who deserve to receive nothing. Do you also notice in several of those verses that there are different measures of grace? If grace were only forgiveness of sins, we'd all have the same measure of grace. We need more grace for bigger callings and bigger temptations. Let us pursue greater grace!

The law of "Try Harder" says, "I need to be stronger to be free… I need to be better or different or more holy or more…" Grace gives us the ability TODAY to say, "I am free from this sin because of what Christ has given me by grace; and I have the ability to overcome temptations because of what Christ can do through me by grace!" In the past, I often thought that I needed to be stronger to resist the attacks of the enemy. That attitude was a great cop-out - nothing more than a way to pardon my falls until some magical future day when I feel like I have "arrived." The Bible, however, teaches that we overcome the desires of the flesh by walking in the Spirit - God's power operating through us(Ga. 5:16); and furthermore, that our strength is in the Lord and in the power of HIS MIGHT (Eph. 6:10). To perfectly resist the enemy in our own might, we must ourselves be perfect. But in grace we realize that we can never in the flesh be perfect and thus we can stop chasing the wind and start to walk in the reality of the new man who is NOW both acceptable to God, and through our acceptability in Christ, able to receive access to all heavenly blessings and Christ's ability to overcome the sin that we cannot.

I can never be wise enough, knowledgeable enough, strong enough in and of myself to defeat a smarter, tireless spiritual foe. I need to walk in Christ's strength IN me which comes by grace. Through grace you have all the freedom, power and revelation to overcome sin that you'll ever need. Pride goes before a fall, the Bible teaches. Conversely, to know that you have to be 100% empowered by God and that He gives you the victory is true humility. If you start relying on anything else and giving glory to anything else, whether it has been 2 minutes or 20 years since you last fell, you are an open target for the enemy. But know that if you should mess up and sin, it is grace again that gives access to divine forgiveness and restoration. So it is by grace we are freed and by grace we fight.

You don't need a mountaintop experience with God to be free. There is no mountain higher than Christ's ascension to Heaven where He constantly intercedes for you so that His ability and righteousness can be manifested in and through you. You need active grace giving you what you need today to overcome the conquered sin that still resides in the flesh and walk as the new man He created you to be. You need the grace of God to be poured out into your life, in every area of your life, at every moment of your life. Period. No matter how strong you are, there are stronger temptations. If you know 1001 tactics, the enemy will find a temptation for the 1002nd tactic. If you have a 12-step program mastered, the devil will trip you with a 13th step.

Grace doesn't mean you won't fight battles and face terrible temptations. The enemy will be relentless and constantly change his tactics. The fact that we will face persistent, gut-wrenching struggles is why we can't do this without grace. We must develop a lifestyle that is interwoven with walking in the Spirit: allowing God's gracious divine guidance and empowerment to guide, fill and provide for our needs in every moment. When we ask God for revelation, really we should ask that God would grant us grace that we should be able to receive His thoughts and ways. When we need strength, we really need grace that we should be able to receive divine impartation of strength. Christ IN you is the hope of glory (Col 1:27). When we minister, our attitude should be like Paul's, who over and over said that he was a minister according to the grace of God that was upon Him.

When you really begin to understand your complete and total poverty of spirit apart from the Grace that has come to you according to the mercies of Christ it will revolutionize your life. A man who is 100% convinced that he is incapable of doing anything great or miraculous apart from God will give God ALL the glory when he is used. The man who is 100% convinced that if he is tempted today that he will ONLY NOT mess up if God's grace is upon him will begin to walk in victory. Until the day this world is done and the devil and his messengers are cast into the lake of fire, the only freedom that is real is that which comes by grace. If grace, that is God's manifest ability and power is not empowering you, the devil can and will find a way to tempt you, torment your mind, deceive you and cause you to fall. So let us be men who are strong in the Lord and in the power of His might. His might in me is mightier than all my best intentions, efforts and any might that I can conjure up on my own.

WORKBOOK MATERIALS

Reflect and answer the following questions from this week's study.

SELF-EXAM

1. Have you ever beat yourself up after messing up?
2. Have you ever felt too dirty after messing up to run to God?
3. Does your sin ever make you feel disconnected from God?
4. Do you feel like you need to "clean up your act" for God to fully love and accept you?
5. Have you felt like God is angry with you because of your sin?
6. Have you felt a weight of shame over your life when you think about your sin?
7. Do you have a hard time forgiving yourself/loving yourself with this sin in your life?
8. Do you/have you felt like God has abandoned you in your struggle – i.e.: do you feel like you have to fight this battle and win it on your own?
9. Do you feel like you can or should try harder to fight your battles?
10. Have you ever felt unqualified to serve God or minister to others because of your sins?

How does this new understanding of grace change the way you think about the above questions? How will this change of heart affect how you live and relate to God?

_____

_____

_____

_____

_____

_____

WORKBOOK QUESTIONS FOR REFLECTION

1) Before you read this chapter what definitions have you heard and what was your understanding of Grace?

_____

_____

_____

2) How would you define grace now?

_____

_____

_____

3) Why do you think we so often beat ourselves up when we sin?

_____

_____

_____

4) How does the following scripture teach us we should respond when we mess up?

For godly sorrow produces repentance leading to salvation, not to be regretted; but the sorrow of the world produces death. For observe this very thing, that you sorrowed in a godly manner: What diligence it produced in you, what clearing of yourselves, what indignation, what fear, what vehement desire, what zeal, what vindication! In all things you proved yourselves to be clear in this matter. - 2 Corinthians 7: 10-11

_____

_____

_____

5) Think about the statement "If YOU are disappointed in YOU when YOU mess up, it was YOUR strength you were relying on." How do these emotions of Godly "sorrow" differ from ways you've felt about yourself in the past after messing up?

_____

_____

_____

6) How do you need to change the way you think and feel when you have blown it to begin to walk out "Godly Sorrow"?

_____

_____

_____

7) What do the following scriptures teach us about God's attitude toward us when we are struggling or weak?

For we do not have a High Priest who cannot sympathize with our weaknesses, but was in all points tempted as we are, yet without sin. Let us therefore come boldly to the throne of grace, that we may obtain mercy and find grace to help in time of need. - Hebrews 4:15-16

Therefore He is also able to save to the uttermost those who come to God through Him, since He always lives to make intercession for them. - Hebrews 7:25

_____

_____

_____

8) What do the above scriptures teach us to ask for when we are struggling?

_____

_____

_____

9) Based on the following passages, or some of the passages listed in the Workbook reading, what are some of the things we have access to through grace?

And God is able to make all grace abound toward you, that you, always having all sufficiency in all things, may have an abundance for every good work. -2 Corinthians 9:8

Having then gifts differing according to the grace that is given to us, let us use them: if prophecy, let us prophesy in proportion to our faith; - Romans 12:6

And of His fullness we have all received, and grace for grace. - John 1:16

Let your speech always be with grace, seasoned with salt, that you may know how you ought to answer each one. - Colossians 4:6

_____

_____

_____

DAILY EXERCISES

Every morning during your prayer time, take 5-10 minutes to get grace for today.

A) Ask Him if there are any temptations you will face today or if there are any weak areas that the devil can exploit today.

B) Acknowledge your weaknesses before God & ask Him for the grace that you shouldn't be tempted beyond what you can bear.

C) Ask Him for the way of escape and for the grace to not fall in those areas.

Daily you may face temptations. Grace doesn't mean you won't have to fight or face temptations - rather you receive the victory through Christ rather than through your efforts when you do.

D) When facing temptations, put on your grace identity. Confess that you are now a child of God and you have the victory already.

E) Confess your own weaknesses to God.

F) Ask God to give you the victory for this temptation through His grace. Ask the Holy Spirit to win this battle THROUGH you.

G) Ask God what you have to do to overcome this temptation. His grace has an answer for you.

PRAYERS

Sample prayer of repentance:

Father, forgive me for the times I've walked in self-abuse, guilt, shame and other negative emotions. I was not walking in Your amazing grace but listening to lies about myself. I don't want to do this on my own any more. I repent for the pride of thinking that I can do anything on my own. I repent for the pride of trying to "clean myself up" before I'd be acceptable to you. I reject these attitudes NOW in Jesus' name.

Thanksgiving - running to the Throne of Grace:

Picture yourself standing before the throne of God. How do you feel as you picture Him looking at you? Begin to picture yourself as the redeemed son of God that you are. Know that even now Jesus is interceding for you so that you may have confidence in your acceptability before God. Let this mental exercise be the fuel for a prayer of thanksgiving for the great grace the Father has given you.

Sample prayer: receiving empowering grace:

Lord Jesus, grant me the measure of grace that you have reserved for me – even increase that measure of grace now.

Grant me the grace to break all identification with my past and see myself in a new way – not as a slave to this sin and darkness, but as a Son light and of God. Give me grace to not be tempted beyond what I can bear. Amen.

Sample prayer when facing temptation:

Lord Jesus, You were tempted in all ways just like I am. But You never sinned. I need you to live through me now with that same power over sin and the craftiness of the enemy. Please grace me with the knowledge of what I have to do to overcome this struggle and grace me with the power to perform what You tell me to do. Amen.

Week 2:
The Lesson of Love

OPENING PRAYER:

Father, You are the potter I am Your clay. I give you my mind, heart and body to mold. Grant me the grace right now to hear only Your truth and to be transformed. In Jesus' name, amen.

Going Deeper:
Additional Teaching for Deeper Reflection

The root issues that keep us bound to lust and pornography are rooted in the basic human needs that arise from our love needs: need for love, need for acceptance, need for intimacy – or based in wounds of the heart caused by lack or inappropriate love (which we'll get into later) – masculinity wounds, inadequacies, etc. Therefore, as we start to receive God's love, it destroys the high place of counterfeit love that lust fills in our heart. This takes time; but as we experience more of the genuine love that God has for us, not only will it expose lust as a cheap counterfeit, but it will disarm the lie that somehow we are "sacrificing" something by cutting lust from our lives. As we receive real love from God, this then becomes the entire platform for true freedom that comes from within. Perfect love will disarm all lies. The number one thing that keeps us from being able to receive God's love is shame. As shame leaves, love enters in.

Mirror Exercise

Before you read on, get up and go take a look in the mirror for this exercise. Really, take a couple minutes and do this. Take a good look at yourself. What do you see & how do you feel about the person you are looking at? If you are like most people, you probably are quick to find all of your imperfections and things about your body and looks that you don't like or love. Maybe you see the hurt in your eyes and shame from all the years that you have lived as a shadow of the person you'd like to be. Who IS this person standing in front of you and how do you feel about him?

Here's your next mirror challenge: tell yourself that you love and accept yourself JUST the way you ARE right now - imperfections, sins and all! For many of you reading this, I may as well have just asked you to jump to the moon… an impossible feat. You see, we are all highly trained in agreeing with the enemy's lies. So much so, that the truth of our acceptability and lovability before God can SEEM like more of a lie than the actual lies of the enemy we have believed for years.

Now close your eyes and picture yourself standing before the throne of God. How do you feel when the Lord looks at you? Do you feel affirmation and love pouring from Him or do you have guilt and shame overshadowing you? What would you say to Him if you really were in His presence? What are you wearing in His presence? Do you picture yourself dingy and dirty like the prodigal son on his journey back to his father's house? Or do you picture yourself with the royal robes that the father put on his son; wearing the ring of authority that the father put on the son's hand; wearing a crown because God has made you a king and a priest?

People say, "You don't know what I've done. You don't know who I've become. God can't forgive me - at least not until I change." To think this way is to say that little you has actually managed to do something that the rest of the human race has never been able to do: single-handedly exhaust God's inexhaustible love and mercy. You've managed to find a new category of God's wrath despite the fact that Jesus became the object of 100% of God's wrath. Think about this: when we call someone a sex object, they are degraded and by the very definition of that label "good for one thing only." But we, as the objects of God's love are set before the whole host of heaven and made a spectacle of shock and awe at the depths of the riches of God's love (Col 2:15, 1 Cor. 4:9). The "dirtier" the sinner, the more that all of Heaven stands in awe and worships the Father's capacity to love. Think about that: the dirtier you are, the more all the host of Heaven and the spiritual realm gasps with shock and awe at how amazing the Father's capacity to love His children - when you run to God, angels can't help but worship God! What shall we say, then? Should we sin more so that God get's more glory for His immeasurable ability to love us? Even though that is possible, the effect of this love on the human soul has the opposite effect. It causes us to be built up, changed and positioned to reciprocate that love to God. **The love of the Creator of love creates CAPACITY to love within us as He manifests His love toward us.** *"We love Him because He first loved us"* (1 Jo. 4:19). We can't even love until we receive it by grace! But when we do... it creates a paradigm shift; and we can start to see ourselves as God sees us.

"I am beautiful." "I am loved." "I am a child of God." "God loves me AS MUCH as He loves Jesus." "I don't have to get it right to be acceptable." "I am righteous." "I am free." "I am a great man." Try saying these positive statements out loud as you look yourself in the eye. Are they painful to say? Do they feel like lies? They will until this love begins to take root in the heart. Each statement above has scripture that affirms it as truth... but we are used to hearing the lies the devil whispers about us; and we have subconsciously agreed with those lies so frequently, that the truth even seems like the lie when it first comes from our lips. However, as we agree with the truth and see ourselves through God's eyes, it gets easier and easier, more and more freeing.

Here is another thing to try. Read that list of affirming statements again and take them as truth by faith. Did they get easier? Did they empower you at all? We need to stop trusting what the enemy tells us and start acting on what God has said. Every time you are tempted to beat yourself up; every time you are tempted to think things like, "I'm ugly. I'm stupid. I'm lazy. I'm never going to be free. I'm never going to be righteous. God doesn't love me. I'm a failure. I don't have what it takes, etc." STOP IT! Don't listen to LOVELESS LIES any longer. If you have to speak the truth 1000 times before it starts to feel real, do it.

We need to stop walking in lies and start living in the freedom of who we are. So much of our struggle with lust is because we feel unloved and unlovable; and we feel unloved and unlovable because we agree with the lies that tell us this. It is these feelings that cause us to run to sin to escape feeling this way or to meet love needs that aren't being met... and it is these feelings that keep us FROM running to our loving Father to receive what we actually need. It is easy to run to something dirty when we feel dirty. Then we feel dirtier than ever, need love more than ever, don't feel worthy of God's perfect love and run to sin all over again. When does this cycle end? Now!

THE FIRST QUANTUM LEAP TOWARD FREEDOM is NOT when you stop struggling, but when you start to trust God's love for you is UNFAILING so that you don't struggle with condemnation, guilt and shame when you mess up. Can you see that if you aren't struggling with these, you are becoming FREE on the INSIDE – and **that freedom HAS to work its way out!**

When you believe you are worthy of love and the object of God's love, something amazing happens - you actually begin to be able to RECEIVE love. Until that happens, you subconsciously REJECT love. Paul preaches in Ephesians 3:17-19 that *"Christ may dwell in your hearts through faith; that you, being rooted and grounded in love, may be able to comprehend with all the saints what is the width and length and depth and height— to know the love of Christ which passes knowledge; that you may be filled with all the fullness of God."* **Paul teaches that the foundation of love provides the access point for ALL the fullness of God to enter into our hearts.**

Becoming rooted and grounded in love is foundational to freedom because this gives you the ability to start having your heart's true needs identified and filled by God; it gives you something real to fight for; it changes the way you see yourself... love changes everything.

Most men want to get free because they feel like to do so will gain them the love and acceptance their hearts are longing for. If they get free, they'll feel like "real men." They'll have confidence and self-esteem. If you identify with any of these thoughts, REPENT. It is 100% pride! You can't take your value from something that YOU do. Your value is set by a higher power.

Really, we don't fight FOR acceptance, worth and love, we fight FROM acceptance, worth and love. Your commitment level can never exceed your love level. Love is our launching pad not our landing pad, our beginning not our goal. This is the proper order to get blessed and to launch into freedom. If you have been doing it the other way around, your whole world is upside-down. As you begin to agree with the love of God for you, you'll also see that love start to affect every area of your life. Great things are to come.

WORKBOOK MATERIALS

Reflect and answer the following questions from this week's study.

SELF EXAM

1. Do you ever feel like your sin makes you less lovable?
2. On a scale from 1-10 how much would you say you love yourself?
3. Do you feel like you would be able to love yourself more if there were things different about you (either physically, mentally or spiritually)?
4. Do you ever feel unworthy of God's love?
5. Do you feel like you are a disappointment to Him?
6. Do you ever feel like God has only condemnation for you?
7. Have you ever felt like your sexuality was somehow broken, making you unacceptable?
8. Does your heart always feel like there is something missing or not good enough?

The questions above obviously help us identify areas where our struggle has affected our perception of self-worth, lovability and has allowed shame and condemnation to begin to affect our relationship with God. These are important areas in our heart to address and repent of. Any time we agree with thoughts and views of reality that aren't Godly or Biblical, we should repent and ask God to help us think in a new way.

How does this session's teaching about God's love and the knowledge that you are a heavenly object of His love begin to change any of these views about yourself?

_____

_____

_____

WORKBOOK QUESTIONS FOR REFLECTION

Reflection: Excerpt from the Mighty Man Manual:
My self esteem had been so hurt and continued to be so demolished by the porn addiction that I didn't feel acceptable to God. I saw myself as a tarnished, dirty vessel. The way I felt about myself was that I could never love myself as long as this sin was in my life... so I assumed that God felt that way too. It wasn't a conscious thought, but in my heart I was believing, "If I can only stop sinning like this, then God will love and accept me more.

1) Reflect on the above passage from the MMM. Can you relate to this? Why or why not?

_____

_____

_____

2) Think about and list some of the times when you are susceptible to thoughts of lust and temptation. Do you think that feeling unloved, rejected by God or people, or other emotions such as loneliness or doubt of God's desire to come through for you can influence any of these times? How do these times of weakness relate to your need for love?

_____

_____

_____

3) Think about some of the people in porn or in life that you have lusted over. Try to apply these lessons of love to them and see them as a person who, just like you, needs real love - not a counterfeit. How does God feel about them; and how can this view change the way you see them and keep from using them as objects for your own gratification?

_____

_____

_____

4) Many of us have prayed for freedom so many times that it feels like God isn't answering our prayers or has abandoned us. What would happen if God were to set you free from this while you still believed that your actions make you less loved, less valuable or less acceptable to God?

_____

_____

_____

5) Why?

_____

_____

_____

_____

6) Think about the following statement from the MMM. How does this analogy relate to how you see yourself; and how does this view create a "vicious cycle"?

"Have you ever seen someone spill something on themselves and hear them say, "I just washed this shirt!"? If they had a dirty mouth or a dirty shirt it wouldn't *have been a big deal to get it dirtier. If you see yourself as pure, you won't want to get dirty."*

---

7) Think about what the following scriptures tell us about God's love.
"But God demonstrates His own love toward us, in that while we were still sinners, Christ died for us" - Romans 5:8
"For I am persuaded that neither death nor life, nor angels nor principalities nor powers, nor things present nor things to come, nor height nor depth, nor any other created thing, shall be able to separate us from the love of God which is in Christ Jesus our Lord." - Romans 8: 38,39
Does sin compromise the depths to which God loves you either before or after salvation?

---

8) Think about the following verse. How much sin would it take to exhaust God's mercy?
"Oh, give thanks to the LORD, for He is good! For His mercy endures forever." - 1 Chronicles 16:34

9) Read and meditate on the following verses spoken by Jesus:
John 15:9: *"As the Father loved Me, I also have loved you."*
John 17:23: *"I in them, and You in Me; that they may be made perfect in one, and that the world may know that You have sent Me, and have loved them as You have loved Me."*

What do these verses reveal about how much the Father and Jesus love you?

_____

_____

_____

10) How did the above verses and the mirror exercise from the Going Deeper portion of this workbook begin to affect your understanding of God's love for you this week? Are you beginning to see yourself differently as well as the way God sees you differently?

_____

_____

_____

DAILY EXERCISES

A) Speaking God's truth/Mirror Exercise: It may feel like a lie at first, but as we confess what the Bible says about us, we are training our mind and soul to agree with God instead of the enemy's lies. You may not have time to speak each one of these declarations out every day, but speak out the following list and especially declare the ones that have the most impact and meaning for you every day. Say them by faith until the truth starts to take root. Look in the mirror, reject any negative thoughts about yourself and say:
- "I love (your name) and I accept myself today."
- "I am accepted by my Father."
- "I have God's approval already."
- The God who loves me will NEVER leave me or forsake me.
- I am God's Son. I am not forsaken. I am not abandoned. I am not a bastard.
- God has loved me every day of my life.
- God rejoices over me – God sings and dances over me.
- He rejoiced on the day of my birth - Even right now, God is rejoicing over ME.

- I make my Heavenly Father proud.

All of these statements are Biblically based. Add your own declarations from verses that speak to you about God's love and identity for you. It is time to start rehearsing and believing the truth!- Use any other Biblical verses and declarations that you may want to confess.

B) Casting Down Wrong Thoughts: Every day you will face many thoughts that challenge your self-worth and Biblical identity. Don't agree with them - speak out Godly truth. If you are unhappy with your physical appearance or anything else about yourself, every time those thoughts arise say, "I love (your name). I accept myself the way I am today because God loves me with all His heart this way."

Again, it may feel like a lie at first but it will begin to sink in and destroy the lies of the devil. Do this for any negative thought. If you sin in any way and you are tempted to condemn yourself say, "God loves me! I forgive myself right now!"

We must not only break the cycle of shame this creates in our hearts, but we must become certain of God's love for us in an experiential way. Many of us struggle with things like sin, self-destructive behaviors and body image as an outflow of not experiencing total intimate acceptance and love from God. What's worse, when we choose not to accept ourselves the way we are, we are creating a scenario where God is unable to help us because to do so would be to reinforce the idea that we are unlovable until we change. This would be worse than to leave us with our issues. So use these exercises daily and break agreement with all self-deprecating, anti-love feelings and thoughts.

C) Loving Others: The next time you are tempted to lust after a specific person, take a minute and reflect on the fact that this person is loved enough for God to die for them. Instead of seeing her as a lust object, choose to see her as if she were your sister or daughter just as God wants to save her and make her a sister in the faith. She has a calling, a gifting and a role in the kingdom that is being exploited. Try praying for her and agree with the truth by saying, "I don't lust after her. She is God's daughter. I choose to protect her. She is my sister. I forgive her. I forgive myself. I choose love even when it costs."

D) Receiving Love: Time in God's presence is what changes us. As we receive His love and see ourselves through His eyes, we are given greater capacity to love and to receive love. Start today and make it a point every day to spend time in prayer without a "prayer agenda" - that is to say, take time to simply meditate on who God is and ask Him to minister to you about His identity and calling for you. Mix it up - take different passages of scripture that may speak to you about God's nature or His view of you and meditate on them. Ask the Holy Spirit to give you deeper revelation and understanding of these scriptures and the virtues they reveal. In time, this type of daily quiet time and reflection will be one of the most treasured times in your day and a power tool in your arsenal of tools for spiritual growth.

PRAYERS

This is one of the most important prayer sessions in the whole book. Prayerfully consider the following sample prayers and make them your own with God.

Sample prayer of repentance from false agreements:
God, your love for me is bigger than I know. Forgive me now for all the times I've rejected Your love, Your Word and have believed lies that steal the truth of Your love and of my identity in Christ. I want to start to walk in this love. Please give me the grace of true repentance from this and the grace to receive the depths of your love right now. I also repent for not loving myself. Your Word tells me to love my neighbor as myself and I have despised and rejected myself. I choose

to start loving myself now because you love me. I choose to forgive myself because You forgive me. In Jesus' name I pray, Amen.

Receiving John 17 Love:

Father, Your Word says that You love ME as much as You love Jesus. I choose to agree with your Word by faith now. Say OUT LOUD, *"God, You love me as much as You love Jesus!" "Jesus you love me as much as the Father loves You!"*

You may want to stop and ask if that is difficult to say and believe – Pray it again and again by faith until it starts to sink in!

Letting Love In:

Our feelings of unworthiness cause us to reject the things that God is saying to us to build us up in His love. The things God says about us are so extraordinary and so wonderful that we think, "That can't really be God speaking to ME." It is time to stop rejecting the good thoughts that God has for us. God wants to speak affirming words to us every day in His still, small voice just as we "hear" the thoughts and lies of the enemy about us. We often reject the good thoughts and things that we "hear" from God because we filter out the good because of our shame. Don't let shame and condemnation be a wall between you and God. God wants to speak to you... and you want to start to hear what He says!

Pray this prayer:

"Father forgive me for not being open to the things that You may have been whispering to my heart about your love for me and my worth. Please open my ears to hear Your words of love for me again. I'll receive anything You have to say to me. Would You speak to me right now? What would You say to me right now?"

Now WAIT a few moments and pay attention to your thoughts and listen? Did God give you any positive, affirming thoughts? Receive them! We accept the thoughts of condemnation so easily. Accept God's thoughts toward you now. Write down what He said here. Keep these words and treasure them. Don't let the devil steal them! Make this type of exercise a habit!

_____

_____

_____

_____

_____

_____

_____

_____

_____

Week 3
Shame

MIGHTY MAN MANUAL READING:

Chapter 6 - Understanding the Nature...

Chapter 7 - Destroying the Foundations of Shame

OPENING PRAYER:

Father, You are the potter I am Your clay. I give you my mind, heart and body to mold. Grant me the grace right now to hear only Your truth and to be transformed. Teach me the ways that my heart relates to You through shame and deliver my soul. In Jesus' name, amen.

GOING DEEPER:

ADDITIONAL TEACHING FOR DEEPER REFLECTION

I love the story of Hosea. God tells the prophet Hosea to go and take Gomer, a prostitute, as his wife to create a picture of how God chooses us while we are yet sinners. That alone would be an encouraging tale. But the story doesn't end there. Gomer, like every sinner, eventually discovers that she isn't perfect and she foolishly returns to prostitution and a wilderness of her own making. But something amazing then happens in the story. God tells Hosea to go find her and bring her back. Yes and amen! God wants us back even after we have wandered - but that still isn't the best part! God doesn't tell Hosea to scold her or *demand* her return. He doesn't condemn her, shame her or make her feel like trash and remind her that she is in the gutter. Rather, Hosea seeks her, finds her and PAYS HER WAGE! Did you get that? He's her husband, not some John who has to pay to get a trick. If anyone had a right to demand her for free it is Hosea. But he pays what she's asking to bring her home. Why? Can you wrap your head around it?

The answer is because she has value. She has worth. This is so critical to understand. Lust and pornography is rooted in a lacking love need and low self-worth. This is why to find real freedom, you must first address the love wounds and needs (and why any ministry that doesn't do this cannot possibly bring about true victory). I can't say it better than 1 John 2:5, "But whoever keeps His word, truly the love of God is perfected in him." If God's love has been fully formed in your heart, you WILL walk in the truth; you will know your value; you will know the value of others; you will have the love of God as a precious treasure that is so worth keeping in purity. It is impossible to treat someone like a sex object if you place a value on their worth as an individual. Furthermore, it is impossible to look at people this way if one truly has a revelation from God of their own worth and value. **It is impossible to devalue yourself and trade the glory and grace of God in you for something worthless if you really knew your own worth.**

47

Until that love goes deep, the cycle of shame only makes this problem worse. Men with this lacking love need fold like a two dollar suitcase when temptation arises because they have no reserve in themselves from the cycle of defeat that has raped their souls; and in turn, each defeat diminishes more self-confidence and hope that they can be free. So after a fall, we beat ourselves up and hope that next time it will be different.

However, as we see with Hosea and Gomer, God's path - the first step in breaking the cycle - is to first reinforce your value - to root and ground you in love. Everything that God does builds us up. He will never bless something you do that reinforces a more damaging self-perception. You won't find freedom, real freedom, from this while you have a low self-worth. That's backward thinking. You need to settle the matter of your value, settle who you are in Christ, learn to love yourself today even with all your flaws and get a revelation for God's love and approval for you. Mighty man, you matter to God. I can't say it enough: the reason men try and fail over and over is because the proper foundation based on a personal revelation of God's love is never laid.

Tips and tactics and ten step programs by default cause us to look at ourselves and try to find what's wrong so that we can fix it. Right there is a problem: when you go on a witch hunt in your heart, how can you NOT stir up the very sense of lack that is so characteristic of the stronghold of shame? Tips and tactics can never change the heart or address the root issues behind the actions. Remember, the power for victory comes from the Spirit of God IN you - not from your mental or physical strength. When our eyes and confidence are in the right place, Christ's strength, it will flow through us easily.

Most Christians are trying to live the Christian life without Christ. Sure, we'll go to church and talk about God. We'll pray (even sometimes when we don't need something from God). But I'm talking about the 24/7 co-laboring, love-walk with Christ. I'm talking about the Christian who loves to pray because they know that God loves to hear from them; and they hear from God. They approach God with unwavering faith, based in His word that He will answer prayers and perform EVERY promise of scripture. Christ prayed that we would be one with the Father in the same capacity, in the same way that Jesus is One with the Father. That is so hard to fathom; and I don't presume that I have completely or ever will completely arrive at the full depths this revelation... but I've left the shores at least.

SHAME, UNBELIEF AND FAITH

Unbelief is at the heart of nearly every breakdown of the Christian faith... and shame is at the heart of nearly all unbelief. When we are moving in unbelief, we doubt God in some way. We doubt His word's truth. We doubt that doing what He commands will pay off. We doubt that He'll come through for us. The question is, "Why?" Why would a person doubt? We don't really doubt that God is who He claims to be. Rather we doubt that He really loves us enough, cares about us enough to come through for us. Why? We look at ourselves and how we fall short. We conclude that we aren't good enough, righteous enough, special enough, loved enough or perfect enough for Him to move Heaven and earth on our behalf. We see past failures and train our soul to use them as evidence that we'll fail again or won't measure up again. That is the voice of shame. Shame steals intimacy and freedom.

However, faith is the substance of things not seen and the evidence of things that are coming into reality (Heb. 11:1). By faith we lay hold of the promises of God and see them transform us. The goal of these last four weeks, but more importantly, the goal of all Christian sanctification, is that we should completely destroy every trace of the old man and any residual identity with him, replacing our identity and self-image fully with who we are in Christ. "*I have been crucified with Christ; it is no longer I who live, but Christ lives in me; and the life which I now live in the flesh I live by faith in the Son of God, who loved me and gave Himself for me* (Ga. 2:20)." We do see this heart change by spending time with Him, reflecting on His word and meditating on his character. The Bible tells us that as we behold Him and His glory we are and will be transformed into His very same image from glory to glory by the Spirit of the Lord (2 Cor. 3:18)!

As this identity change takes place, it will radically change the way you act. You will find a righteous indignation rise up in you that will defy every lie of the enemy. When the devil wants to tell you something negative about yourself, you immediately are armed with God's truth about yourself. When you are tempted, you immediately realize that you are better than that sin; that others involved are God's precious ones also. God isn't looking for people with a strong body or a strong will, but for people through whom His Spirit may move in power - people who will live and move and have their being and confidence fully in Him.

God has forever settled the issue of sin and repaired our access to Him. As we settle this fact once and for all, as we are free in His presence, we discover another powerful element to being delivered from shame: His delight. It is one thing to know that God accepts you based on the work of Christ. It is another thing altogether to know that He truly delights in you.

THE DANCE OF DELIGHT

David, our model mighty man from this chapter had a unique perspective on the Lord. Over and over he would talk about how the Lord was his delight; how he delighted in all God's law and word and statutes. David delighted in the Lord because he knew the Lord delighted in him. "He also brought me out into a broad place; He delivered me because He delighted in me (2 Sa. 22:20)."

Did you catch that? How did David come to realize God deliverance? Because he realized the Lord's delight in him! David didn't suppose that God delivered him because he did something right. David didn't pray and fast to see God's deliverance. He didn't do works of penance. He didn't think that God delivered him because of his own righteousness. As a point of fact, when God moved David from the wilderness to the palace in one day, David was living in open rebellion to the word of the Lord and lying daily. Amazing grace!

In Deuteronomy 9:6, God admonishes the people, "Therefore understand that the Lord your God is not giving you this good land to possess because of your righteousness, for you are a stiff-necked people." A few verses later He says that they were still rebellious even to the day of the promise being fulfilled. God brings us to the place of brokenness where we can see the gravity of our sin and our inability to save ourselves. Then He gives us a revelation more powerful than the strength of our sin: His saving grace and love! The result is a people who fall on their face in gratitude and fall radically in love with the One who loves them radically! When you really get this, then, like David, the Lord will be your delight and you will be His.

How much do we delight to run to God? How much do we delight in prayer and reading the word? How much does meditating on God and His nature thrill us? There is a connection between shamelessness and delight. We wrongly think that our sin keeps God from being able to delight in us. However the Word says, "For whom the Lord loves He corrects, Just as a father the son in whom he delights (Pr. 3:12)." When does a father correct his child? When the child is misbehaving, right? So look at that verse again. The Father is correcting us in our misbehaving at the same time as He delights in us. Awesome! Sin doesn't change how the Father sees us. He knows every component of our personality, how He made us, how He called us. He delights in us deeply. The Bible says that He actually sings and dances over us (Zep. 3:17). We sing songs in church about God singing and dancing over us. But have you ever actually pictured God to be so enthralled with you that He, the God of all creation, can't help but sing and dance with delight?

In Proverbs, we hear one of the few passages where the Holy Spirit is speaking in the first person, "Then I was beside Him as a master craftsman; And I was daily His delight, Rejoicing always before Him, Rejoicing in His inhabited world, And my delight was with the sons of men (vv. 8:30, 31). The Spirit's delight is in us; and gives us the capacity to delight in Him. This "dance of delight" is always growing and going deeper. As we experience the delight of the Lord for us, we delight in Him more, which allows us to experience more of His delight... On and on it goes and will go for all eternity; but what a blessing to know His delight now.

As you meditate on God's delight for you, you will find that you love and accept yourself more. You will love your unique gifts and calling more and more. You will fall more and more in love with Him. "Yes, the Almighty will be your gold And your precious silver; For then you will have *your delight* in the Almighty, And lift up your face to God. You will make your prayer to Him, He will hear you, And you will pay your vows... He shall pray to God, and *He (God) will delight* in him, he shall see His face with joy, For He restores to man His righteousness (Job 22:25-27)." This is a powerful promise. God uses this mutual delight, this intimacy without shame to restore you to righteousness and joy.

Do you understand why it is so important to have this foundation of love laid so firmly? This truly is the key to walking in freedom from sin and in the fullness of your calling. If you will make love your pursuit AND your reward, you will find a freedom like you have always dreamed.

BREAKING THROUGH INTO LOVE

As we wrap up this teaching on shame, a few points should be made, repeated and rehearsed for final clarification. We say in the MMM that shame is the fear or expectation that something is wrong with you. Shame creates a heart that is unable to receive God's love because it actually refuses love, despite being desperately needy for it. Shame will always give a reason why you haven't earned the love or aren't good enough for it. Shame is pride-based. It looks at ourselves and what we have or don't have, what we've done or haven't done rather than look at

Christ and His all-sufficiency. Shame, therefore causes us to identify with our carnal self rather than our spiritual self.

If you want love to break through in your heart, you have to settle the following by faith and rehearse it until it dictates your reality.
-   We are saved by grace, through faith and not by works
-   The righteousness that we maintain is also not by works but by the righteousness of Christ imputed to us
-   You have the perfect Holy Spirit living in you now. Your sin can't make the Spirit sinful, so that righteousness can never be diminished = you will never be more perfect in God's eyes than you are today.
-   Your carnal flesh and mind is no more able to sanctify your soul and bring about holy living than it was able to save you when your first came to Christ. How can something unclean make something clean? Only the cleanliness of the Holy Spirit now working in you can clean your heart and actions.
-   Therefore, our relationship with God isn't affected when we fail, because it was never our role to clean ourselves in the first place.
-   The only thing that is affecting your relationship with God is how you PERCEIVE His feelings toward you.
-   If you take the heart of God as represented in the Bible as truth, you can be fully free before God and love yourself today without shame.

WORKBOOK MATERIALS

Reflect and answer the following questions from this week's study.

SELF EXAM

1. In the past, have your felt as if your urges made you unacceptable to God?
2. Have you ever prayed for God to take away your sexual urges?

3. Have you ever begged God for something or fasted, hoping that you could "convince" Him to give it to you?

4. Have you ever felt unqualified or that God can't use you for great things?

5. Do you spend much time in prayer and eagerly expect that God is answering your prayers.

If you answered, yes, to any of the questions above, they indicate that shame has been a key factor in how you relate to God and see yourself. The purpose of this time of reflection is to let the truth sink in and allow your soul to begin to receive God's love apart from shame.

1) In the past, when you would see a beautiful woman how would you respond? How has the instruction in Chapter 6 changed the way you respond to or will respond to beautiful women?

_____

_____

_____

2) When you are exposed to temptations that have a mixture of beauty and natural attraction and the exploitation of beauty or some manner of lustful or sexual perversion, what is the two-fold response that you will need to remember from James 4?

_____

_____

_____

3) Does this new understanding of your sexuality help you feel more acceptable before God? Why or why not?

_____

_____

_____

4) Do you feel more free to run to God even after sinning in various ways now?

_____

_____

_____

5) List some ways that approaching life from the attitude of HAVE vs. HAVE NOT will change your confidence and expectations.

_____

_____

_____

_____

_____

_____

6) Have you ever stopped to consider God's delight in you? How will knowing God's delight change the way you live?

_____

_____

_____

CONFESSIONS OF FAITH

Make the following declarations aloud. See how their Biblical truths begin to affect how you see yourself as you make them repeatedly:

- I am saved by the blood of the Lamb
- I am fully righteous
- God's goodness is better than all my badness
- I can't out-sin the mercy of God
- My sin can't make the Holy Spirit dirty
- The Holy Spirit's holiness makes me clean
- I am a son of the living God
- My old nature is dead

- I have all things that pertain to life and Godliness
- I am good
- I am better than sin
- God delights in me
- God rejoices over me
- I have a future, hope and a calling
- It's not about me
- Even when I sin, none of the above changes
- I am free today. Praise Jesus!

7) As you make the declarations above, do you find it gets easier to relate to God and love yourself? If you picture yourself coming into the throne room of Heaven, do you feel that your attitude is different now?

_____

_____

_____

PRAYERS

Freedom From Sexual Shame:
Father, I've believed that You couldn't accept me with my sexual urges. Thank You that Your goodness is better than my badness. Forgive me for how I've used the sexuality and sex drive that You gave me for sin. I repent. I know that I have a sex drive to serve Your purposes and in so doing I bring you joy as a Father. I choose to use my sex drive and my body as You designed, not for sin and self-gratification. Please help me when tempted next time to identify with You and not with my old, dead nature.

Prayers for dealing with attraction:
Lord, I confess that I've felt feelings of attraction to _____ and I've not dealt with them in a proper manner. Forgive me for any sins of fantasy or lust that I've entertained concerning this person. Now I choose to repent and deal with these

feelings in a Godly way. Lord, this person is extremely beautiful. Thank you for giving them the gift of beauty. I am blessed by their beauty and I'm so glad that I can appreciate beauty without sinning. Thank you that my sex drive and soul are working exactly the way You designed them to work and here shall the temptation stop.

(if the person above is flaunting their sexuality or behaving in a seductive or perverse way)

I reject their spirit of seduction, lust and perversion. You may not devour me with it; and I will not devour them in lust. Father forgive them and set them free from their bondage and agreement with this sin. I take a few minutes now and ask You, Father, to give me Your heart for them and to show me how I can pray for their salvation and deliverance.

Deliverance from shame after sinning:

Lord, You know my sin; but I know that it didn't take You by surprise. It didn't change the way You feel about me. Therefore I come boldly and gladly to Your throne of grace. You are still for me. You still love me. You still live for me. Your goodness and mercy know no end; and this sin doesn't change that fact. I praise You for Your love. You restore me, by the blood of Jesus to righteousness. You make me whole again. You called me a prince and a co-heir with Christ. I will forever now live as the man I am, rather than the man I was. I will leave no provision for this to take place again. In some way I began to trust in myyself rather than in your grace and Spirit bringing the victory through me. I repent and pray for the gift of full repentance. Perfect Your love in me. Amen.

Receiving God's Freedom:

Lord, You love me. You don't just love me, You DELIGHT in me. Thank You that I am free to be me when I talk to You. You take the good, the bad and the ugly in me and conform me into Christ's image. You are my life. You are my reward. I now reject all shame and any spirits of shame that have kept me bound to sin. I receive Your unconditional love now and for the rest of my days. Amen.

Week 4
From Head Knowledge
to Heart Knowledge

MIGHTY MAN MANUAL READING:
Chapter 8 - Getting Ready to Face Your Demons
Chapter 9 - Sowing and Reaping in the Fear of the Lord
Chapter 10 - Where there is no Vision...

OPENING PRAYER:

Father, You are the potter I am Your clay. I give you my mind, heart and body to mold. Grant me the grace right now to hear only Your truth and to be transformed. In Jesus' name, amen.

GOING DEEPER:

ADDITIONAL TEACHING FOR DEEPER REFLECTION

The goal this week will be to really clarify the truths that govern your life and actions and, by the grace of God, allow them to deeply impact the way you think and act. As you have, no doubt, already experienced in the weeks leading up to this, temptation doesn't take a vacation because you determine that you are planning a life change. Quite to the contrary.

The devil may be a lot of things: a liar, a thief, a killer, a destroyer... but he isn't a bad business man. He's always ready and willing to pull the wool over your eyes and make a cheap trade. There are a lot of lies we accept that cause us to fall prey to temptation, but I think one of the devil's favorites is the lie that sin doesn't cost us anything but "gives" us something; and nothing could be further from the truth.

There is ALWAYS a trade-off for sin. EVERY time you choose to lust you are losing something. Joshua said it this way, *"I call heaven and earth as witnesses today against you, that I have set before you life and death, blessing and cursing; therefore choose life, that both you and your descendants may live"* (Dt. 30:19). We lie against the witness of heaven and earth when we think that our sin is inconsequential or has no lasting ramifications beyond the moment we wash our hands of it. If we were Adam in the Garden of Eden, one slip of our sin alone would be enough to curse all the earth and creation... but somehow we think that sin is casual and won't affect the microcosm of our lives.

Yes, the devil does a good job throwing temptation in our face and saying, "Look at what you are missing. You need this." And when it is all said and done, we feel as though sin is an *"opportunity"* to be grasped as opposed to a shabby, worthless, life-stealing trade. **Defining our vision, training our mind with what we are fighting for and getting real with blessing and cursing - these truths need to become a part of us so that we understand what we are putting on**

59

the table for this trade so that we can make an informed decision the next time satan wants to offer us a shiny new deal.

There have been many, in fact, countless times that I have come face-to-face with temptation and everything in me cried out to gratify that temptation, but knowing that there are consequences to sin, not wanting to suffer loss and a desire to fulfill my life's vision kept me from gratifying that temptation. Whereas I realize and confess that this mindset is based in selfish motives, Isaiah gives us a dose of reality when he tells us that ALL our righteous deeds are like filthy rags before God - always tainted with impure motive. So we choose to do what is right, knowing that heart change is a journey and trust that God will, by His grace, work out impure motives in due time as He changes the heart. He leads us first by the hand and then by the heart as we prove what is the good, perfect and acceptable will of God by working it out and seeing it in action. This is far better than waiting around to get perfect before we get serious about departing from iniquity; and far better than walking in ways that "reduce a man to a crust of bread" and "destroy kings" as the Bible teaches.

This is as real and as practical as it gets at this stage of the journey. There are consequences in heaven and earth for what we do - both spiritual and tangible. At the very least, we know that by walking in sin we have sacrificed precious time, seared mental pictures into our mind, reinforced a horrible habit and opened doors to deepening perversion. At worst, we hope that we have not sacrificed something greater or find ourselves at the place where God starts to deal severely with our iniquity and allow us to eat the fruit of our own ways as the Bible teaches.

Many men have lives that are highly devastated by this sin. It is heartbreaking to know that your sin has wrought destruction in your life - and to fall again despite knowing this. But there is hope. The book of Hebrews teaches us that God chastens every son whom He loves. If fact, the scriptures teach that if God DOESN'T chasten you over sin, that you would be an illegitimate son. That means if there is chastening in your life, God loves you and only has allowed it to serve the purpose of allowing you to awake to the fact that the wages of sin is death; to allow you to awake to the fact that your life has purpose and that He wants to help you. Chastening isn't a bad thing. The first chapter of Proverbs PROMISES that if you will turn at the Lord's rebuke, surely He will pour out His spirit on you and CAUSE His plans to be made known to you. So we are both blessed as beloved sons and chastened as beloved sons. Chastening doesn't mean that God is angry or has turned His back on you... it means He loves you and is calling you back to your high place in Christ. Becoming rooted in this sonship love is critical to our confidence before the Throne of God when circumstances and feelings tell us to wallow in self-pity rather than re-embrace our identity, love and position in Christ.

I'm convinced that part of our problem as men of God in the first place is that for the most part, day-in and day-out we don't live our lives as though they have meaning or purpose... or we are living mostly for ourselves with little thought using our time, gifts and resources to help and bless other people. Is it any wonder that when the enemy offers us an opportunity for a purely selfish, self-gratifying act we are quick to snatch it up?

If you really want heart change, you need to get deadly serious with what you are really living for and why. The three chapters for this week's reading serve as a powerful 3-part foundation. Part 1 - we know that we will face strong temptation until God's work in our heart truly sets us free. Part 2 - we develop a clear vision for our lives that clarifies what we are fighting for with a deep conviction that we MUST walk in freedom today. Part 3 - we know the fear of the Lord and accept the fact that tolerating iniquity will inevitably cost us the very things that we are fighting for. So utilize these tactics and allow God to root them in your heart as they will serve you countless times while on your journey to deepening freedom in the heart.

WORKBOOK MATERIALS

1) Read the following story from Genesis 25:29-34.

Now Jacob cooked a stew; and Esau came in from the field, and he was weary. And Esau said to Jacob, "Please feed me with that same red stew, for I am weary." Therefore his name was called Edom. But Jacob said, "Sell me your birthright as of this day." And Esau said, "Look, I am about to die; so what is this birthright to me?" Then Jacob said, "Swear to me as of this day." So he swore to him, and sold his birthright to Jacob. And Jacob gave Esau bread and stew of lentils; then he ate and drank, arose, and went his way. Thus Esau despised his birthright.

What lessons can we learn from this story as we relate to our own fleshly struggles?

_____

_____

_____

_____

2) Read and meditate on the following scriptures and answer the following question.

"Where there is no vision/revelation, the people cast off restraint; But happy is he who keeps the law." - Proverbs 29:18

"Her uncleanness is in her skirts; She did not consider her destiny; Therefore her collapse was awesome." - Lamentations 1:9

"Looking unto Jesus, the author and finisher of our faith, who for the joy that was set before Him endured the cross, despising the shame, and has sat down at the right hand of the throne of God. For consider Him who endured such hostility

from sinners against Himself, lest you become weary and discouraged in your souls. You have not yet resisted to bloodshed, striving against sin." - Hebrews 12: 2-4

What do the above passages teach us about the importance of developing a larger, spiritual vision for our lives?

_____

_____

_____

_____

_____

3) What do the following passages indicate about the importance of rehearsing God's Word and the truths that we want to govern our lives?

1 My son, keep my words,

    And treasure my commands within you.

    2 Keep my commands and live,

    And my law as the apple of your eye.

    3 Bind them on your fingers;

    Write them on the tablet of your heart.

    4 Say to wisdom, "You are my sister,"

    And call understanding your nearest kin,

    5 That they may keep you from the immoral woman,

    From the seductress who flatters with her words.

- Proverbs 7

"Write the vision And make it plain on tablets, That he may run who reads it." - Habakkuk 2:2

_____

_____

_____

_____

4) Consider the exercise at the end of Chapter 13 about vision and truth. If you have not done so already, prayerfully consider and write a list of all the truths and reasons you want to and HAVE to be free from this today.

_____

_____

_____

_____

_____

_____

_____

_____

5) Reflect on the passages below and answer the question that follows:
"For by means of a harlot A man is reduced to a crust of bread; And an adulteress will prey upon his precious life. Can a man take fire to his bosom, And his clothes not be burned?" - Proverbs 6:26-27

Excerpt from the MMM: *"Did God or His character change? No. Did I deserve what I was reaping? Yes. Suddenly I was very sober about my sin. I thought, "Maybe I should start to watch my speed." God wasn't cursing me or waiting to smite me... my own sin was reaping its consequences and God simply had to remove the grace, take a step back and let me begin to eat the fruit of my own ways."* - MMM, p. 107

Consider these laws of sowing and reaping. Prayerfully consider and write a list of all the things that lust addiction is stealing in your life.

_____

_____

_____

6). Now look at your two lists above. Think about times when you may have fallen and how you were thinking or lies you may have believed that allowed you to depart from God's truth. Do you have things written on your lists above that are Godly truths that combat those lies?

_____

_____

_____

DAILY EXERCISES

A) Take time each morning to prayerfully consider times you may be vulnerable that day. Ask God for the grace to not be tempted beyond what you can bear and By His grace working in you, visualize and resolve how you will react to those temptations before they happen.

B) Meditate on your lists this week. Ask God to give you DEEP conviction regarding these truths. Be prepared to use them to counter lies the enemy puts in front of you.

C) Caution - don't think that you can mentally beat a spiritual problem. This is why we stress prayerfully allowing God to work these truths and visions into your heart. Allow your vision to be a work of the Spirit and not a mantra or carnal crutch.

PRAYERS

Sample prayer of repentance:
Lord, I have treated Your Word and Commandments as a light thing. I have not honored You or Your Word. I have lived as though sin is an inconsequential matter and I now repent. I ask You for the grace to love You with ALL my soul, ALL my mind and ALL my strength and to have no other gods before You. I have traded Your truth for worthless things. I have said with my mouth that I love You, but with my actions I have chosen to serve my desires above Your Word.

I give You my heart now Father and I turn my back on anything that would take Your place. In Jesus Name, Amen.

Strengthening convictions in your heart:

Take out your lists. Ask for the grace that these truths should become more real to you than the lies and temptations you face. Go through each item on your list and ask God to write this truth on your heart and into the fabric of your life.

Prayer of Sonship:

Father, You have loved me with an everlasting love. You have welcomed me with open arms despite my sins against You. You have crowned me with loving kindness as a good Father. Even if I stray, even if I feel abandoned, You chasten every son you love. I receive your loving correction. I rejoice in a long life walking side-by-side with You, my loving Father.

Dealing with Curses and Curse Theology:

Many of you have been wrongly taught just as I was that our sin has given the enemy "legal space" to curse us. In fact, for years and even in previous editions of the Mighty Man Manual and Workbook, I taught this same prevalent curse theology – which is really a mixture of Old Testament Law and New Testament grace. I was wrong. However, we can rejoice in the fact that Jesus has fulfilled the Law and become a curse for us, once-and-for-all. We therefore no longer need to break every curse of the Law individually and live in fear of them coming back on us every time we sin. Rather, we rejoice in the fact that God, in His wisdom, created a Covenant where we can be delivered from oppression even if we aren't perfect.

What we actually must repent of is every agreement with the belief that our sin is more powerful than the sacrifice of Christ – for putting more faith in the old, dead Law than we do in the teachings of the New Testament which clearly and consistently state that the Law's power over us is cancelled. It is not our sin that brings curses – but what we've been wrongly taught and believed about curses that re-empower curses. When the enemy comes with his bad theology and says, "See this Old Testament Law – it says that your sin gives me the power to curse you, doesn't it?" It is our AGREEMENT with the lie that our sin brings a curse that re-empowers the dead Law and provides the "disarmed" enemy with fresh ammunition to again enact curses in our life.

If you have been taught this, prayed along these lines and lived in fear that your sin is bringing about curses in your life, the New Testament answer is incredibly simple: Every curse of the Law has been broken; every righteous requirement of the Law fulfilled; every enemy disarmed; and you can enjoy FREEDOM as it was meant to be enjoyed! In the New Covenant, we break curses by breaking AGREEMENTS that empower the enemy:

Father, thank you for sending Jesus to pay my price, to completely fulfill the Law that I never could. Thank you for destroying every curse of the Law when you cancelled the handwriting of requirements that were contrary to me and in so doing disarmed the powers and principalities. Thank you that the enemy can no longer bring a curse or charge against God's elect. Thank you that I deserve only what Jesus does – blessing and favor that follows me all the days of my life!

I repent for believing that my sin is more powerful than Christ's ability to deliver me from it. I thank You that I am curse-proof in Christ! Forgive me for any ways that I have re-enacted the dead Law and opened a door to cursing in my life. I now consider myself dead to the Law in Christ and resurrected to new life. I now embrace the cross as my all-sufficiency; I receive my inheritance as a co-heir with Christ and the blessings of my new spiritual heritage as a son of God and heir of Abraham's blessings. Thank you Jesus!

Week 5
Spiritual Warfare and
Thought-life Victory

(This section won't deal specifically with chapters 11 and 12 but we recommend reading them as you go through the MMM)

OPENING PRAYER:

Father, You are the potter I am Your clay. I give you my mind, heart and body to mold. Grant me the grace right now to hear only Your truth and to be transformed. In Jesus' name, amen.

GOING DEEPER:

ADDITIONAL TEACHING FOR DEEPER REFLECTION

If you plan to change the way you act, you have to change the way you think and what you think about. From the moment you chose to follow God, you have been at war. Even beyond this sin, there is a constant war in the spiritual realm that we must learn to fight. Therefore, these lessons on spiritual warfare and thought-life victory will become very familiar, essential daily practice. We daily put on our armor, we do drills and exercises and we fight battles. Thankfully, heart change comes in due time.

Spiritual Warfare 101: the battleground

One of the most difficult things for me as I came out of a lifestyle of lustful iniquity was how to deal with incidental, accidental and the everyday temptations that we may come across in a lust-fueled culture. The typical sensual scene in an "innocent movie;" the image search on the computer that yielded an unexpected porn image; the girl in public flaunting her body, etc... these all presented their "opportunity" to my flesh and could leave me yearning to run back to the old, familiar, carnal crutch.

We live in a culture where the idea of fleeing from lusts as the Bible teaches will only get you so far because lust is EVERYWHERE in our society. We are out of places to flee and we must learn how to fight. Exposures to temptations of lust that find us in nearly every unexpected corner of our lives present themselves as "opportunities." And they are - they are opportunities for our flesh. But know this: **every opportunity to feed your flesh is also an opportunity to feed your spirit!** You can either have a strong Spirit and a weak flesh or a weak spirit and a strong flesh. The Bible teaches that your flesh and your spirit are at WAR and can never be reconciled. *"For the flesh lusts against the Spirit, and the Spirit* *against the flesh; and these are contrary to one another, so that you do not do the things that you wish"* (Gal. 5:17).

Your Spirit and flesh are locked in a diametrically opposed battle royal. Your mind, thoughts, emotions and the soul are stuck in the middle of this war; giving us the ability to be carnally minded or spiritually minded, a proverbial tug of war over our soul, each mind-set, each kingdom trying to pull the soul into its camp of victory. *For those who live according to the flesh set their minds on the things of the flesh, but those who live according to the Spirit, the things of the Spirit. For to be carnally minded is death, but to be spiritually minded is life and peace. Because the carnal mind is enmity against God; for it is not subject to the law of God, nor indeed can be... For if you live according to the flesh you will die; but if by the Spirit you put to death the deeds of the body, you will live. For as many as are led by the Spirit of God, these are sons of God.* Romans 8: 5-7, 13-14 (cf. 1 Peter 2:11). Furthermore, the battle is exacerbated by the forces of the spiritual realm also waging war through your thoughts and emotions against the Spirit.

But praise be to God when you realize that you are in the middle of this battle. Because where the devil's "opportunity" to the flesh seems irresistible when it appears to be the ONLY opportunity presented to you in the heat of the moment; when the lie is exposed and you realize that you also have a more glorious opportunity in the Spirit for EVERY opportunity for the flesh, we now have the ability to choose the life of God and know what we are fighting for! **Furthermore, we understand that the path of God's grace or divine empowerment isn't directed at making the temptation go away, but rather is empowering us with might through the inner-man so that we can resist and destroy the works of the devil.** And so we, the mighty men of God can and must awaken to the realities of the spiritual warfare going on around us 24/7 and put on our spiritual armor and begin to dispossess the devil of his territorial gains, first in our hearts, then our families, then spheres of influence and eventually the world.

One of the devil's favorite ploys is to get us to live as though he doesn't exist or influence our daily activities. I've even heard churches preach that the devil was defeated at the cross and doesn't have any more say in our lives... If that were the case, then why do almost all of the New Testament books, which were written after the cross, teach us about the realities of spiritual warfare and its role in defeating the enemy? Don't get me wrong, there is a lot of strange, unbiblical practice on this subject in Christianity. However, let's not throw the baby out with the bath water: we MUST live a lifestyle of spiritual warfare and defeat the works of the devil.

Spiritual Warfare 201: Discerning of Spirits & Spiritual Warfare

Before we begin this teaching, let me demystify the concept of discerning of spirits. There is a lot of weird practice in some Christian circles. The teaching you'll find in this section is pretty practical, non-mystical and, for the most part, requires nothing more than good, old-fashioned common sense to employ. That being said, the Bible does teach every believer to test the spirits. 1 John 4 says, *"Beloved, do not believe every spirit, but test the spirits, whether they are of God; because many false prophets have gone out into the world. By this you know the Spirit of God: Every spirit that confesses that Jesus Christ has come in the flesh is of God."*

OK. Let's "un-weird" and demystify that passage. Most of us have never had and probably will never have some spectral phantasmagoria appear to us like the Ghost of Christmas Past, giving us cause to dust off this passage and ask it the all-important question of whether it names the name of Christ... so what does this challenge to "test the spirits" look like in every-day, normal Christianity? The passage above states that every spirit that confesses or testifies of Jesus is of God. In John 15:26 we read that (no surprise) the Holy Spirit is the Spirit that testifies of Jesus: *"But when the Helper comes, whom I shall send to you from the Father, the Spirit of truth who proceeds from the Father, He will testify of Me."* Furthermore, we know that the Holy Spirit bears the

FRUIT of the spirit (Love, joy, peace, patience, kindness, goodness, gentleness, self-control, faithfulness (Gal 5:5). The fruit of the Holy Spirit looks a lot like what we would call "emotions." Therefore, we simply understand that through normal encounters with the Holy Spirit, we will experience His spiritual fruit - (peace, joy, patience, kindness, self-control, etc). These are the emotions that are produced as a byproduct of His manifestation.

The Holy Spirit is not the only spirit that leaves "fruit" as a byproduct of its operation. We understand that a spirit – good or bad – bears fruit which we discern as EMOTIONS. If you are angry, frustrated, fearful or feeling in any way that is counter to the fruit of the Holy Spirit, the most practical thing you can realize is that your emotions are the **testimony** of another spirit at work against you bearing bad spiritual fruit. Therefore, the most practical way that we test the spirits is by using our natural common sense to gauge our thoughts and emotions to evince the activity and work of the enemy against us. **If our emotions testify of the Holy Spirit at work, we are walking in the Spirit. But if our emotions are negative, we know another spirit is working in us and we must begin to fight our way out of its grasp.**

When we understand that ungodly emotions are the fruit of spirits, we realize that spiritual warfare is far more necessary than we ever realized. This is immensely practical advice as we apply it to our sin and struggles. You will find that often, your weaknesses are precipitated by emotions that act like trigger points for your soul to run to lust as a coping mechanism. For me, frustration, feeling overwhelmed or purposeless were "spirits" that would take me into a downward spiral that would eventually lead to a fall. But being able to test the spirits, recognize their work against me and stop thinking like a devil before that mental track would take me somewhere I didn't want to go was critical to winning battles.

This simple understanding of spiritual warfare is a powerful tool with application that goes far beyond this struggle with lust. **Too many**

Christians wrongly think it is OK to go through their lives accepting ungodly thoughts as normal. Whether these people are "demon possessed" or "demonically oppressed" is an argument within Christianity that has taken us away from the real issue: dealing with the stinking devil and his influence.

Christians often go through their day and lives feeling unhappy and depressed; go through life hating themselves or parts of their body; are OK with holding grudges and with unforgiving attitudes against others; having arguments or fights in their head over conversations or events that are in the past (or that never actually even happened); fantasizing about lust or ungodly things; frustrated or short tempered and justifying a bad attitude; unloving; riddled with low self-esteem; and the list goes on and on.

Let us illustrate this point with depression for a minute. The Bible commands us to rejoice at ALL times – even during trials and persecution. But most people and even Christians don't think there is anything WRONG or sinful with feeling depressed despite the fact that these depressed thoughts, feelings and actions run contrary to the direct commands of scripture listed above as well as countless other scriptures. Depression is SIN and opens doors to other sins and spirits! When we feel depressed and don't do anything about it spiritually, we AGREE with it, accept it as normal and often wait for IT to change rather than changing it. The devil has duped us into passivity and spiritual victim mentality. This is the wrong way for a Christian to live their life. WE are the ones to dictate how we feel and what we believe – IN EVERY AREA OF THOUGHT, WORD AND ACTION! The emotions and "spirits" that you tolerate will dominate and affect as many areas of your life as they can.

Christian men go around tolerating fear, depression, hopelessness, defeatist mentality and a host of clearly demonic mindsets and wonder why we aren't beating our habits. We are waiting around for our feelings to change so that we can finally start living the victorious Christian life. This is completely backward.

God has called us to be masters of our emotions and thoughts, to take thoughts captive, to destroy the works (the fruit) of the enemy... this is normal, everyday spiritual warfare and normal Christianity. Not every EMOTION you feel is valid or permissible. Not every THOUGHT you think is your own. The enemy will hang around as long as you'll let him, whisper in your ear and manipulate both your thoughts and your emotions. You have to recognize when these attacks are taking place and destroy the works of the enemy!

The devil always tries to drag you down to a vulnerable place in your emotions. The devil tries to put thoughts in your head hoping that you will agree with them, think they are your own nature and that maybe you'll feel better tomorrow - all the while giving him a deeper and deeper foothold until it becomes a stronghold as the Bible teaches.

We have to REJECT every thought that doesn't line up with what God's word says about us! We have to stir ourselves up and REJECT every emotion that isn't a fruit of the Holy Spirit.

And so we understand that 99% of the spiritual warfare we face as Christians takes place in the normal, daily war for our mind and emotions that is constantly taking place. Furthermore, the Bible says that the truth sets us free. 99% of the spiritual deliverance and freedom that we experience as Christians takes place as a result of learning and meditating on the Word of God, applying its truths to our lives, thoughts and emotions and allowing the Holy Spirit to work those truths deep within us. Thus the truth exposes the lies, disarms them and takes their power away forever.

Use this practical principle to easily identify when you are thinking and feeling thoughts and emotions that require casting down and taking captive. Knowing is half the battle and when this spiritual discernment becomes normal and natural so that the devil can no longer lie to you and make you pretend that he isn't there, you will be well on your way to winning your battles.

Spiritual Warfare 301:

Thus far, our engagement with the enemy has been defensive, how to parry his attacks as they come against us. What we must understand is that this isn't how God intends spiritual warfare to take place. Rather, we are commissioned to destroy the works of the enemy, to be a city on a hill, the light of the world that dispels the darkness. We are not called to merely site in our safe ivory towers and defend against a skirmish here or one there; but we are to tear down the strongholds of the enemy.

What America learned in the Vietnam War is that that it isn't enough to win a battle and then simply move on; it isn't enough to take a hill one day and expect it to stay "taken." One of the factors that cost America that war and untold life is that we failed to hold down and occupy a territory after we had taken it. The enemy simply moved back in after we left. Then to our surprise, when we needed to move back through these areas, the enemy had re-occupied and was again entrenched. We are seeing the same thing happen in Iraq. As we prematurely remove our military presence, conflict is again erupting, causing a political dilemma of whether or not to reenter and re-engage to re-secure what we fought for in the first place.

Jesus warned of this phenomenon in spiritual warfare as well. In Matthew 12:44, He explains that if all you do is cast out a devil but do not fill the place it left, it will not only return, but will bring reinforcements, leaving the state of the man even worse. I fear that what isn't being taught in spiritual warfare is that you must, not only defeat the enemy but occupy the stronghold after it has left. Too many Christians lose and grow weary in warfare because we simply kick out the devil over and over and leave a void in the soul unsatisfied.

In the Mighty Man Manual we talk about overcoming a "have-not" mentality with an attitude of abundance. We talk about the importance of not merely trying to not sin. ANY lie, any agreement, any attitude, any emotion, any space occupied by the devil must be replaced with godly attitudes and emotions. For example, if God gives you the grace to recognize that you have a poverty mentality, it isn't enough to simply break agreements with that. You must form new agreements with God's Word. You must embrace new attitudes. You must choose to entertain new emotions that line up with the Word of God. It isn't enough to simply not have a mentality of lack; if you don't develop a Biblically-based mentality of abundance, you will never occupy a place of abundance and depose the despot of poverty. This principle holds true no matter what the stronghold may be that you must destroy.

In this way, we understand that warfare isn't defensive, limited to defending against attacks, but offensive. We don't just have spiritual armor; we have a Sword of the Spirit. The skirmish battles that come against us only serve to awaken us to the fact that there is a stronghold that we must discover and destroy. It isn't enough to settle for a lifestyle where we are winning the same battles time and again. To have true victory spiritually we must tear down the entire stronghold that gives the devil space to keep tempting us in an area in the first place. To do this, in the midst of battle, God must help you gain revelation as to WHY this temptation has space in your heart. What is the root of the thing? What are the core lies you believe? What are the agreements you have in your heart? What is the counterfeit or substitute that you are accepting in place of the real thing?

THIS is the heart of the matter and the thing that drives us deep into intimacy with God through warfare. The goal of ALL the Christian experience, including spiritual warfare, is intimacy with God! The entire purpose of man's creation in the Garden was for intimacy. The entire aim of Christ's sacrifice was to restore Immanuel-God-with-us fellowship. **If you miss this point, you miss the point of all spiritual warfare and will ultimately fail at it.** ONLY God can reveal these root issues; and only God can actually fill the space and meet the true needs that are being masked by sin.

I remember for most of my life, I had similar scenarios play out time and again where people I loved and trusted would reject and wound me. When I broke all agreements with rejection so that even if people did reject me, I didn't *feel* rejected or agree with the lie that I was a reject, everything changed. Until that point, I had a rejection wound that the devil kept taking advantage of through other people. The truth was that in my heart I also believed I was rejected by God. My soul feared that the Holy God could never truly love and accept dirty Jon. But when my soul came to know that, even at my worst, I'm as loved and accepted as I ever can possibly be, I stopped being a reject. I became "bullet-proof" to rejection. It is no coincidence then, once rejection was healed in my heart, these cyclical circumstances of earthly rejection also ceased. Why? The devil isn't going to waste his time or resources with something that has no benefit to him. A wise soldier isn't going to shoot a pellet gun at something that is bullet proof. That would be an exercise in futility and a waste of ammunition. Likewise, when the agreements and strongholds are removed from your heart in any area, the devil isn't going to waste his time tempting you because he knows that he can never again cause you to stumble in that area.

To tear down strongholds, we must consistently wage war against the attacks and temptations, but more importantly, develop the relationship with God that helps us discern the agreements that make us susceptible to those attacks in the first place. I heard a preacher say "You can't stop birds from flying over your head… but you CAN stop them from nesting in your hair." This funny little statement is a good analogy to the warfare that goes on in our thought-life. The enemy comes along with a thought or a temptation flying around in your mind and hopes that you'll let it land and settle. The Bible tells us to take these thoughts captive. When we simply ignore ungodly thoughts they linger. When they linger they gain power. As they gain power we begin to agree with them. As we agree with them we are conformed into their image and a stronghold forms (Rm. 12:2). Let us rather be TRANSFORMED by the renewing of our mind and thoughts in Jesus!

The thoughts you tolerate will dominate. Winning thought-life temptations takes action. When you encounter an ungodly thought, impure memory or soul tie you must reject it as from the enemy. But more importantly, you MUST change your mind, draw near to God and access the grace to think His thoughts instead. The Bible tells us what we should be thinking instead of the wrong thoughts. Each time we wage war against wrong emotions and thoughts we take back some of the space that the enemy once occupied. Eventually we push him all the way back to his bunker, the lie at the heart of the matter. We must, in many cases, stand on truth time and again until God begins to reveal where the entry point is for the enemy so that we can break the wrong agreements based on lies we've embraced. These lies are the "strongholds" that the Bible speaks of when talking about spiritual warfare. We must tear down the strongholds and make agreements with God so that He can take up residence in the areas once occupied by the enemy.

If the temptations persist, ask God even to speak to you in the moment if there is anything you need to do or what you need to transform your mind. The presence of the Holy Spirit IS the evidence of grace upon your circumstance that brings victory with each temptation; but moreover, when you become familiar with your thought life and the issues surrounding your various times of temptation, you'll begin to understand the heart issues - what you really need and why the devil's counterfeit seems to be attractive - so that Jesus can heal the heart and set you free. Therefore, this session really is the transitional gateway from "sin management" to true victory!

You may have days where the battles seem endless. You may find yourself rejecting some thoughts and drawing near to God in prayer for grace all day. Good! Consider this your time of combat training! Big battles produce big champions for God. If you never had to fight a battle, you'd have very little spiritual strength and character.

Learning to master your thought life and take thoughts captive as the Bible teaches is a learned virtue that becomes natural as you take more time to pray, meditate, think and reflect. In teaching prayer classes at my local church, I often get the comment, "I can't pray because my mind races, bounces from thought to thought and I get too distracted." This isn't an indication that you CAN'T pray, it is an indication that you need to pray MORE - that you don't have enough time to process the 1000 thoughts bouncing around your head when you finally take a few minutes out of your day for God. God wants to bless and be a part of all the things that concern you.

A Christian needs quiet time to be aware of our thoughts, face the issues in our heart, carry them to God and grow. Similarly, when we are being tempted, we need the familiarity with our thought life, the strengthening and mind transformation that only comes from time in God's presence and the familiarity with God's thoughts and Word to understand WHY this temptation is there in the first place. There are so many factors and ways for temptation to enter our hearts. How will you know how to properly respond to temptation if you don't know or understand the nature of the temptation? How will you be able to get the grace and essence of what you need from God if you don't understand the emotional root that gives the temptation "the right" to be there in the first place?

We are so completely dependent upon God for everything. Our culture simply numbs us to the reality of this statement. The pain we feel during spiritual warfare is simply the pain of a God-starved soul waking up to its dire hunger and need. Each step away from sinful living needs to be a step toward a closer, intimate walk with God. Spiritual warfare outside of this context of relationship will inevitably turn into a "name it and claim it," false power doctrine that gives the illusion of spiritual growth without the reality of knowing God more and more.

A few words of caution:

When you get close to really tearing down a stronghold, the same thing happens as would happen in a physical war. When soldiers move into enemy territory, the enemy fights back. Intensified spiritual warfare is a strong indicator that you are taking over enemy territory.

As you come out of this lifestyle, especially if it has been a deep, long-term habit, you'll face some pretty intense spiritual warfare and thought-life battles. Junkies and drug addicts have been known to do just about anything to get a fix. Now hopefully most readers of this book aren't in this that deep, but make no mistake about it, even if this is a "casual addiction" there WILL be withdrawal. Do not be deceived. Parasites don't willingly disconnect themselves from their hosts; and the devil likes to feed from you. He will not go without a fight.

Right about the time you start to feel like you have gone longer than you ever thought you would, when you are starting to think, "Wow. I'm really changing," this is right about the time when your thoughts will go haywire and logic, reason, spirituality and sanity will go out the window. You will start to think things like, "I want porn SOOOO badly." "I can't do this." "God doesn't care about me." "My life is worthless." You will feel frustrated, irritable, short-tempered. You will be tempted to look at "lesser evils" or "innocent lustful things" and COMPROMISE. This WILL lead to a fall. Your dreams will be disgusting. You will be tempted to fantasize and tell yourself it is OK. etc... and if you make it through all of that, the enemy will probably shift gears. You'll feel lonely. You'll feel depressed. You'll feel lethargic. You'll feel bored out of your mind. You'll feel like all life is pointless and like there is no joy left in the world. You will face every thought and emotion you can possibly imagine... This is the devil throwing everything he possibly can at you. The only sure thoughts in your head are the ones that line up with the Word of God.

It will get better. Really. That is small consolation during addiction withdrawal. Take my word for it and just assume that when your soul gets very uncomfortable in withdrawal, every thought and emotion in your head will be a lie. Take pleasure in knowing that the enemy is the one truly freaking out that he is losing his grip on you.

A final word of warning about distractions and entertainment. Use entertainment in moderation. To learn to master your thought-life, you have to be familiar with thinking! Entertainment such as TV is proven to reduce brainwave function. This is a perfect time for the enemy to start to plant his thoughts and get in past your defenses. I mention in the MMM that the definition of "amusement" comes from "a", a prefix meaning "against" or "without." And "muse", meaning "to think." So amusement is a way "without thinking" to escape for a while. Most Americans just go from moment to moment automatically bouncing from one form of amusement to the next repressing thoughts and cares and never really growing or processing thoughts and stimulus. Too much amusement and entertainment will dull your mind and spiritual discernment. So do all things in moderation in the Lord.

Spiritual Warfare 401:

I believe the fourth component of spiritual warfare we'll cover in this workbook is the aspect that most people probably think about when they hear the term; but is also the aspect of spiritual warfare that gives it a bad name in conservative Christian circles due to a lot of misinformation and bad practice.

I'm speaking of the practice of directly praying against, binding or casting out a demon, sometimes called deliverance ministry. Many churches who practice deliverance, frankly, give way to much attention and emphasis to the work of the devil. Yes, the devil is real and he does manifest through people. I've seen this firsthand many, many times; and every believer should have at least a basic understanding of what to do when face-to-face with a truly demonized person or situation where spiritual warfare is needed. However, there are the types who are looking for "the devil behind every doorknob" - they are always "binding" this and binding that... but, here's the problem: they do so without REAL, case-specific revelation, real power and real effectiveness.

I'm a firm believer in spiritual warfare, the spiritual realities of binding and loosening and deliverance; but I have also been to countless churches where I come away thinking, "Those people are WEIRD." There are, unfortunately, a lot of Christians with a little information who are doing a lot of damage. It is important to keep balanced in all areas of spiritual warfare and allow these times to flow out of RELATIONSHIP and REVELATION with the Spirit. Jesus modeled a lifestyle where He only said and did what He heard the Father saying and doing. As soon as a believer gets outside of that safety zone, we run the risk of getting a bit off track and can get focused on something that God may not be focusing on.

Still, many have a fascination with these intriguing stories. Every ear perks up when I start to tell stories about times when I've delivered a man writhing like a snake and foaming at the mouth. People want to know, "How do I do that?" The truth is that God probably won't put you in a scenario like that if you haven't been practiced at "normal" spiritual warfare, like we've already read about.

So just to recap, before we move on, what does "normal" deliverance practice look like? First, as we understand that ungodly thoughts and emotions are actually manifestations of spiritual warfare, we broaden the scope of our understanding a bit. Thus, the most typical application that you'll have is during the course of your day as you face various temptations and emotions that are ungodly. As you struggle with these thoughts and emotions that aren't your own, it becomes obvious that there is something present that is trying to influence your actions and take you in a direction contrary to the Holy Spirit's work.

In cases like this, when we clearly see the influence of the enemy we simply can pray something like, "I reject these thoughts in the name of Jesus. These thoughts aren't mine and I choose to think God's thoughts." If it is a negative emotion, "I recognize that this emotion isn't consistent with the fruit of the Holy Spirit. I will not surrender my will to this spirit, in Jesus' name. I will choose emotions that are godly and ask You, Holy Spirit, to work in me now through Your power."

This isn't a formula - simply pray as the Holy Spirit should lead - but do take authority over false spirits and tell these obvious attackers to leave as we have the authority in Christ to do so. You don't have to yell, hop, stand on one foot or feel any particular emotion about this type of warfare - the work is by the authority of Jesus. A private in the army delivering an order from one officer to another doesn't have to be happy, sad, energetic or tired for the order to be effective - the authority exists on a higher plane than his emotions. His attitude only affects his experience in carrying out the order and in his qualification for promotion apart from that assignment.

Sometimes it isn't too clear when there is a spirit at work. In the Mighty Man Manual, I recount a story where God revealed a spirit of seduction in operation. Note one important aspect of that: God revealed it. He also gave the power to take authority over it. The temptation that many face when they hear a story is to assume it applies in every similar situation. It doesn't. When we look at Jesus' ministry, He never healed or delivered two people the same way - even if they had similar manifestations. We need to exercise spiritual discernment in ALL spiritual warfare. Spiritual discernment is gained as we fight our daily battles. One can't ASSUME that there is a spirit of seduction in every case of attraction because they heard my testimony about it. You can't take "authority" over a spirit in Jesus' name that may or may not be there. Again, I can't stress enough that we must employ spiritual discerning in conjunction with spiritual warfare.

I have attended many churches where they are "binding" everything that THEY can think of. I remember a shopping trip with someone once who bound a devil of vehicular accidents over the trip, bound the power of the enemy over their shopping, bound the devourer over their fruits and veggies, etc. I'm not joking. We were walking into the supermarket and they literally started "praying" and binding the devil over their fruit. Not only is practice like this crazy, I'd be willing to bet that through the course of the day, this person would invoke the name of Jesus 100 or more times when there was no call for it.

The reality is that 99% of the spiritual warfare happening around us takes place SOVEREIGNLY. That is to say that God orchestrates our protection against attacks that we could never foresee and would probably mess up figuring out how to fight them anyway. The Bible teaches that He gives His angels charge over us. They are constantly fighting battles and protecting us in ways that we can only imagine. All of this happens without our cognizance and direct involvement. Aren't you glad?

Too many Christians in circles where deliverance theology has grown out of balance are like an army private who hears that there is a battle... somewhere... grabs their gun and goes running off to find it. Zeal is good, but we, as God's soldiers need to wait for the King's orders when it isn't clear what His strategy for the battle will be.

"Name it and claim it" deliverance, trying to manipulate the spiritual activity without revelation and understanding according to what we assume is happening and using the name of Christ to do so is a form of taking the Lord's name in vain! It gives the illusion of authority and power, but doesn't work for us today any more than it did for the Seven Sons of Sceva in Acts 19. In this familiar Bible story, it was common practice in their town to drive out spirits using the name of Christ. But when these characters tried, they couldn't drive out the demons; rather the demons drove THEM out of the town. The Book of Acts equated their use of the Lord's name to sorcery.

Similarly in Mark 9, even the disciples couldn't cast out an evil spirit. Jesus called their attempt to do so apart from intimacy with the Father an act of perverse faithlessness. I've, likewise, watched as half a dozen pastors tried to cast a devil out of a man "in Jesus' name" to no avail. They were doing everything they knew how to do: rebuking the spirit, commanding it to stop manifesting, telling it to come out in Jesus' name, hopping, jumping, yelling... and nothing happened. I went into the midst of the insanity and knelt with my knee in the man's back (because he was convulsing violently amidst other manifestations) and just began to pray, "Father what do You want to do for this man?" I prayed like that for a couple minutes while the others kept doing their name-it-and-claim-it deliverance. Finally, God gave me a word. I didn't need to shout or jump up and down because the command was from the King. I told the man what God put on my heart and he instantly came into his right mind and was healed from an issue from his childhood. He made the comment to me that he was aware of everything happening, but my voice was the only one he could hear. Really, he was just hearing the voice of the Father in me.

If I hadn't developed a lifestyle of personal spiritual warfare through intimacy, this scenario would have played out very differently. Either I would have cowered on the sidelines or have been another among the crowd of those taking the Lord's name in vain. Spiritual sorcery is exactly what the attempt to use the Lord's name to bind and drive out demons without revelation and authority is today. Sorcery is the act of spiritual-realm manipulation apart from the Spirit of God. Slapping the name of Jesus onto human effort to conquer the spiritual realm is a dangerous practice that you should take the time to read about in the books of 2 Peter and Jude.

Therefore let us not fall into that trap, but be led by the Spirit of the Lord. We have a responsibility to bring our thoughts and emotions into alignment with God's word. But beyond that, if you think that there are spiritual forces at work against you but don't have any real revelation, the answer is simple - just pray and ask God to either reveal what you should do or simply ask Him to sovereignly deal with them and deliver you just as He probably is already doing in 1000 other ways at any given moment - He is called the Lord of hosts for a reason - He is the One in command of all the hosts of heaven. This practice will help you keep in balance and is a lot easier than trying to "bind" everything your small, human, 3 pound brain can think of.

Sometimes when we don't see results or we encounter a spiritual need greater than the day-to-day call for deliverance, we simply need to pray, fast and do what is necessary to get the revelation to rise to this challenge. This was Christ's advice to the disciples when they couldn't cast the evil spirit out of the epileptic boy. Remember the model: Jesus had a lifestyle of only doing what He saw the Father do and only speaking what the Father said. When this is our approach, there is no spiritual battle that is too great.

We like to hear the juicy, shocking stories of supernatural encounters people have had while on missions trips. Frankly, overt demonic manipulation of a person is not just isolated to witch doctors in Africa - there are plenty of demonized people in America too. It is always a bit alarming to encounter someone truly demonized or the supernatural. But remember, even these encounters are easily overcome when the Spirit of God is in the lead.

Like all things in the Kingdom, there must be BALANCE. Some camps of Christianity see other groups with a deliverance theology out of balance and they think, "That can't be God." They polarize and go too far in the opposite direction, rejecting ALL spiritual warfare, until they, themselves are out of balance. Relationship with God is the dividing line in all differing points of theology. Your relationship with Jesus will give you revelation and authority if you should face the supernatural in other areas as well. Spiritual warfare can be very effective, normal and practical if you stay focused on God, loving Him, growing in Him, loving your neighbor as yourself and allow Him to do the leading.

WORKBOOK MATERIALS

1) It is tempting to think that because God hasn't completely isolated us from all temptation, that He hasn't heard our prayers to save us from our sins. What reasons can you think of that it is actually a good thing that God doesn't just completely take away all temptation or make us think holy thoughts all the time?

_____

_____

_____

Consider the following verse and answer the questions that follow:
2 Corinthians 10: For though we walk in the flesh, we do not war according to the flesh. For the weapons of our warfare are not carnal but mighty in God for pulling down strongholds, casting down arguments and every high thing that exalts itself against the knowledge of God, bringing every thought into captivity to the obedience of Christ" (vv. 3,4,5).

2) Where and how does the Bible tell us that this battle will be waged and won?

3) According to the scripture above, what are you to do with EVERY thought and feeling that is contrary to the thoughts, works and experience of God?

Consider the following writing and verses and answer the questions that follow:
"You are not who you've been or how you've acted or what carnal devils you've agreed with. You are not a pornography addict. You are not a pervert. You are not any of the things you fear you are becoming. You are a new creation in Christ Jesus. All things have passed away. All things are new (2 Cor. 5:17)! When a lustful or perverted thought enters your mind, that is not you any longer. It is not your nature. It is a devil or at the very least your dead carnal flesh trying to resurrect some old habitual pleasures and bad habits. Count yourself dead to your old nature." - Mighty Man Manual – p. 84:

Likewise you also, reckon yourselves to be dead indeed to sin, but alive to God in Christ Jesus our Lord. - Romans 6:11
But now, it is no longer I who do it, but sin that dwells in me. - Romans 7:17

4) What do the above teaching and verses tell you about your thoughts versus sinful thoughts?

_____

_____

_____

5) How does looking at yourself and your thoughts in the light of those statements change the way you perceive your identity?

_____

_____

_____

6) You will think about the things that you spend time doing and meditating upon. List some of the activities and habits that take up most of your day and free time. How does the amount of time you spend praying, reading the Word and other things that shape Godly thoughts compare? What are some activities that may be out of balance (done too frequently or infrequently)? What ways can you create new habits and start to develop a lifestyle with more of the Word and God's influences on your thought life and Spirit?

_____

_____

_____

_____

_____

7) What are some of the times, feelings or situations that you find make you most susceptible to temptation? List them and then prayerfully consider the following:

- Are there any lies or thoughts from the enemy that are associated with these times of weakness that you can now be aware of and take captive?

- Are there any ways that you can better prepare for that war before it begins?

_____

_____

_____

_____

8) When you find yourself struggling with the same thought, memory, personification of a temptation or soul tie over and over again, what are some of the things you can remember to do?

_____

_____

_____

SELF EXAM:

The thoughts that you tolerate will dominate. The way we think and feel is a powerful component of spiritual warfare. Read over the list of common "spiritual warfare" traps that many people deal with. Often we don't even realize that emotions and thoughts are things that we should reject and be at war with. Check off any of these that you commonly fight and generally don't "take captive."

_____ Feeling Unhappy
_____ Feeling Dissatisfied
_____ Feeling Depressed

_____ Hating things about yourself (physically or
emotionally)
_____ Having a hard time forgiving someone who has
wronged you
_____ Allowing frustrations and setbacks to make you short-
tempered or affect your mood
_____ Being easily agitated or snapping at people
_____ Reliving situations or arguments you may have had
_____ Having "arguments" repeatedly in your head that may or may
not have happened in reality
_____ Experiencing perverse fantasies
_____ Being fixated on a body part or sexual act
_____ Repeatedly fantasizing about a particular person or porn star
_____ Repeatedly fantasizing about a fantasy you may have made
up

All of the above are indicators that demonic forces are present and
should never be tolerated. These different emotions, thoughts and
scenarios all are mentioned in the Bible as tactics of the enemy to tear us
down and steal from us. We will review tactics from the book during the
prayer session that help us deal with these types of issues.

Now think about any other common emotions or feelings or thoughts
that aren't fruit of the Holy Spirit or don't line up with the Word of
God. List them. Repent for agreeing with these ungodly thoughts, and
ask God for the grace to change your mind when they try to bring you
down again.

_____

_____

_____

DAILY EXERCISES

A)   Be conscious of and monitor your negative thoughts. Look at the self-exam list and ask God to remind you when you are thinking these things so you can STOP. What does the Bible say to you about the things on that list? Choose to get God's perspective. Choose to reject the negative thoughts and say, "NO! I reject that thought in Jesus name! You may have to do this 100 times a day until it starts to sink in, but trust me, when it does, you will finally be in a place where God can give you the grace to start to change. Get rid of thinking, "I'll love myself when..." or "I'll be acceptable or better when..." or "I'll be happy & satisfied when..." God has made you acceptable and has given you things to be thankful for today. Start believing Him more than the lies of the devil and you'll be happier and mentally healthier.

B)   Monitor your emotions (test the spirits). Negative emotions are fruits of evil spirits just as the Bible lists positive attributes as fruits of the Holy Spirit (love, joy , peace, patience, self-control, etc.). You don't have to keep FEELING bad any more than you have to keep thinking bad things. When you are frustrated, angry, depressed, etc., reconcile these feelings in God. His Word says He has given us ALL things that pertain to life. Usually negative emotions are based in lies we've agreed with. Ask yourself why you are feeling the way you do and remember you don't HAVE to feel bad just because you are having a bad day. You don't HAVE to be unhappy just because something great isn't happening in your life today. Christians should be the happiest, most free people in the world! We have the most to be happy about! Even on our worst days, we have hope, salvation and a Father who loves us and is working ALL things for our good! When you are reminded that you deserve Hell but won't have to go there; when you are willing to "die daily" to sacrifice anything for God, anything that you have above and beyond that becomes a blessing and a source of true joy.

C)   Monitor your perverse thoughts. Aren't you glad perverse thoughts aren't YOUR thoughts?! If you have been born again, you have a new mind and heart. That junk is just the devil tempting you and trying to make you think you are a sinner not a saint. Reject every perverse thought by saying, "NO! I reject that thought in Jesus name! That isn't my thought. That's the enemy trying to make me think like a devil. I am a Saint and a Son!

D)   Remind yourself every morning that you are a servant of God's who needs grace to fight. Prepare your mind and know each morning what you plan to do when temptations may arise. This is a step of what Paul tells us to do in Ephesians 6: put on the whole armor of God so that you can stand against all the schemes of the devil.

E)   Monitor your soul ties. If you find yourself "haunted" by thoughts of a particular scene, fetish, person or porn star, you may need to break soul ties as it teaches you in the book. Set aside some time to break soul ties with EVERY porn star or sex type/fetish you have lusted after. See if this doesn't give you a measurable level of freedom over the next few days.

F)   Break wrong agreements. Review the story on page 83 of the MMM. One young lady simply spoke out the truth day after day until it broke the belief in demonic lies. Find any area of perversion or escalation that has sunk in where the devil has caused you to believe that YOU think or act that way.   Say, "I reject that lie and the liar behind it in Jesus name. I cancel that lie and the devil's assignment against me right now!" Recite God's truths over you. Find scriptures that speak to you and make them your own. Recite them until you believe the truth more than the lies. You don't have to listen to or believe every thought you think!

G)   Break subtle agreements. As you go through your day, notice all the things in our culture designed to excite lust. In our flesh and carnal mind, the reality is that we ARE tempted and enticed by them. Therefore when we simply ignore these temptations, we have made an agreement that is never reconciled in Christ. Our heart said, "Wow. I want that"... and we ignored that agreement rather than take it captive. This unrepentant agreement will create an open door later. When you see something that creates lust, acknowledge it in your heart and repent for the lust. It is as simple as that. Agree with the truth, "I am a son of the light and not of the darkness. I have no fellowship with lust. I forgive myself and that woman/man for their part in this. I reject the enemy and cancel your assignment of lust against me in Jesus name!"

H)   Get full of the Word & Pray. Set aside time to pray and read the word. Do things that get more of the Word in your heart. Go to church, Bible studies, small groups. Fellowship with strong Christians, listen to sermons online or on your iPod, listen to praise music in the car, watch Christian films or programming. The list is endless... so are the possibilities for the Christian who is full of the Word!

PRAYERS

Sample Prayers of Repentance:

Father, I confess I've believed many thoughts and even lies about myself. I repent. Forgive me for agreeing with the enemy's opinion of me more than Yours. Give me the grace to see myself in the light of Your truths and Your realities. Make Your realities and opinions my realities and opinions. In Jesus name. Amen.

Father, I confess that I have not taken temptations, perverse thoughts, and a host of other thoughts captive that have over and over let my mind and heart away from Yours. I repent. Help me to not tolerate wrong thoughts even for a second. Give me grace to meditate on Your thoughts.

Father, I confess that I've allowed my emotions often to rule me instead of ruling my emotions through partnership with Your Spirit. In so doing, I've agreed with a spirit other than your Holy Spirit. Please forgive me. Give me grace. I break agreement with these spirits now. They never did anything for me. I don't even know why I wanted to walk around with negative emotions. I pray You would help me recognize negative spirits and overcome them by the power and fruit of your Holy Spirit. Amen.

Breaking Agreements:

Review your self-exam from this session. Take some time to specifically pray about any emotions or common thoughts that plague you. Ask God to minister to your heart about these and show you why these are familiar to you. Ask Him to make you aware of these stumbling blocks when they surface and for the grace to deal with them. Ask Him to show you how to "put on" mindsets and actions that will keep these from coming back.

Sample Prayer to Break Soul Ties:

Father, please forgive me for idolatry and lusting after this person. I believed that they would do something for me that they are not created to do. I repent. I forgive them And right now I choose to turn from them and any related idolatry. I break my soul ties with them in Jesus name. I reject every devil or unclean spirit associated with them. I break every spiritual covenant and contract that is formed between me and them in Jesus name. Where my soul idolized them and was joined to them, I worship only you and ask that my soul be joined to Yours instead. Jesus, restore me completely now I ask. Amen.

Week 6
Healing the Heart

MIGHTY MAN MANUAL READING:

Chapter 19: All In All

Chapter 20: Coping Mechanisms of the Heart

Chapter 21: Love one Hate the Other

Chapter 22: A Satisfied Soul

Chapter 23: Trust

OPENING PRAYER:

Father, You are the potter I am Your clay. I give you my mind, heart and body to mold. Grant me the grace right now to hear only Your truth and to be transformed. In Jesus' name, amen.

GOING DEEPER:

ADDITIONAL TEACHING FOR DEEPER REFLECTION

For too long our hearts have leaned on lust and porn as a crutch, a filthy counterfeit for the needs, desires and wounds in our hearts. We run to lust because we feel like we're missing out on something, but really something is missing from us: there is a hole in the heart that God wants to fill and that ONLY God can fill. Victory is all and always has been all about Jesus. As we stop leaning upon lust for a support, we will become those who lean heavily upon the God who truly loves us, knows us and comforts us. To follow after sin will lead you deeper and deeper into corruption of the soul. Similarly, to seek after God will lead you into deepening dependence and love of Him. *"For he who sows to his flesh will of the flesh reap corruption, but he who sows to the Spirit will of the Spirit reap everlasting life. And let us not grow weary while doing good, for in due season we shall reap if we do not lose heart"* (Gal 6:8,9).

The biggest criticism that our ministry hears about the Mighty Man Manual is skepticism regarding this issue of Jesus ACTUALLY healing the heart and setting a person free from lust. Many Christians who are even in "anti-porn" ministries will say that you can never be free and transformed to the point that you have nothing in common with lustful response to temptation. Thankfully, that isn't what the Bible teaches. 2 Corinthians speaks about this type of transformation: *But we all, with unveiled face, beholding as in a mirror the glory of the Lord, are being transformed into the same image from glory to glory, just as by the Spirit of the Lord* (v. 3:18). ARE BEING = present tense transformation into the likeness of Christ as we look at and meditate on Him! Isn't that good news?

The Bible has a lot to say about maturity, sanctification, reaping of the Spirit, growth and the formation of Christ's character in the inner man. All of these concepts are present-tense, ongoing, current realities for the believer according to the working of the Holy Spirit. If we were talking about a "smaller sin," nobody would have an issue with believing for real freedom. Most Christians, for example believe that a person can be set free from telling lies or acting out anger or stealing - even drugs. As a whole, people don't have a problem with these; really that is because on some level people feel it is within THEIR power to control these behaviors. But when it comes to something that many Christians feel is "in their nature" to act some way, they say, "A man can never be free from lust." But guess what? Lust is not in your nature if you have been born again. Your nature is God's nature and as we look upon the living Christ, we are being transformed - that is to say that the old, dead nature is being destroyed by the manifestation of our new one! No sin, big or small, is bigger than our God. It is all about Him! If we have faith to look at the small things and expect Him to work them out, we may as well look at the big sins and expect the same. Praise God! He really did come to heal the broken hearted and set the captives free.

We are the epistle of Christ being written with the stroke of the Master's hand. I'm sure most every Christian can think of many sinful ways they used to think and act before the truth of God and the working of the Spirit set them free. When I look at who I was 10 years ago, I think, "WOW... who was that guy? Was I even saved?" I was just a carnal Christian with a lot of heart molding needed from the Potter. Now when I look back at the ways I used to think, act and react to sexual and lustful temptation, I think, "WOW... who was that guy?" I can no more relate to the "person I used to be" in this area than if I were watching a movie about some guy who was addicted to lust. Today I think differently, act differently and react differently to beauty and sensuality based on the character of Christ being formed in my heart. I look forward to looking back on myself today with changed eyes and thinking, "WOW..."

Therefore we all know that God changes the heart because all of our hearts have been changed in various ways. So we conclude that we must gain knowledge that comes from knowing Christ that we may understand our true nature and not misunderstand what is "normal" and what is a perverse response to normal stimulus. There really are people in the world who don't struggle with lust. If you put them side-by-side with someone who does struggle with lust and expose them to the same "temptation," you would see two very different reactions. They would perceive this stimulus differently, think differently about it, respond differently to it and feel differently about it than you might. So we further understand that a lustful response is not inherent to the human condition but a matter of individual perception. I have heard scholars say that when the Pharisees threw the woman caught in adultery before Jesus they probably didn't clothe her. This could have been a stimulus that would excite a lustful response from someone who struggles with lust. However Jesus, though fully human, a man with flesh and bone, did not respond to this in lust. Therefore, we conclude that, just as we read earlier that it is HIS character being formed in us, we also can look forward to a promise of victory from lust. That is the plan for every believer.

Lust is from the devil; thus it is not NATURAL or NORMAL to lust! We must learn the difference between healthy, normal response to beauty and lust. It is normal to see a beautiful woman and recognize that she is beautiful and even be attracted to her. It is not normal to see a beautiful woman and lust after her. Lust is a dynamic that takes place in the heart that perverts God's plan for beauty, devours a person and exploits their beauty. It turns a human into the play toy of the one doing the lusting and desires that she be thrown away as trash when finished. We see this scenario over and over in porn stars and even in many young Hollywood stars and musicians who get caught up in the vicious cycle of exploiting their beauty in a sexual way to sell more movies and music. Their songs, videos, movies, attitude and attire take them deeper and deeper into lust-fueled lifestyles that the public wants more and more of until their lives burn out. We hear about their drug addictions and breakdowns with interest and fascination... until another comes along after that one has been used, abused and thrown away. This cycle perverts God-given beauty and talent.

The devil always tears down, God's love always builds up. **When you are free from lust, you are free to respond normally and naturally to BEAUTY which is from God.** Response to beauty is built into the human soul. The freed man can see a beautiful woman, celebrate her beauty just as God, her father celebrates her beauty, then direct his heart into unity with God and not have one iota of agreement with lust or the devil; not have one sliver of perversion or wickedness take root. As Christ is continuously formed in your heart, as you become like Him, as He washes you by the washing of the water of the Word, as you become sanctified, you too can be one of those people in the world who don't struggle with lust to the praise and glory of God!

Conversely, lustful response to stimulus is learned and reinforced by heart issues that make us susceptible to temptation. The "normal" response to all ungodly temptation should be shock and either repulsion or a myriad of other Godly responses when we walk in the Spiritual mind. An extreme illustration of this point could be your reaction if someone were to show you a picture of something reprehensible (say, a picture of someone having sex with a pig, pedophilia or a sexual picture of your own mother, etc). Despite the fact that there are people who even get sucked into these types of acts, the normal response to perversions such as these is most often and SHOULD be revulsion. These things are obvious perversions and one would and should conclude, "It is clearly demonic and not normal to be fascinated and attracted to that type of perversion and darkness." The reality is that ALL sex outside of marriage and depictions thereof is a form of perversion that can be as clearly repulsive and dark as what we would consider to be "extreme perversions" as listed above. We need to re-learn "normal" according to God's standards.

When a man's heart beats with God's love for himself and for God; when that man meditates on the things that God loves and aligns his heart with them; when a man sees himself as a new creation and hates the dark things of this world; when a man views porn stars and "sex objects" as children of God, daughters, princesses, sisters, then all forms of porn and lust are exposed as perversions and become vile and untempting. These girls selling themselves can be no more tempting than if you were to see your natural sister trying to do the same thing. You can experience the same indignation and desire to cover those girls as you would for a natural sibling. Perversion isn't natural. It is demonic. For this reason, a man truly CAN be free. When God exposes this reality and the devil dangles some vile "temptation" in front of you, the new man, the REAL you looks at it completely differently than you had in the past. Praise God!

God's plan for heart change:

God promises to heal the corruption of the heart if we will sow to the Spirit. I remember after battling for a long time and not really seeing real freedom, I felt as if God was putting a challenge in my heart: put His Word to the test. Try Him. I knew in my head that "He who is in you is greater than he who is in the world" (1 Jo. 4:4)... but how was that knowledge really affecting my daily life and experience with God? If that verse is true, why did it seem like the world was winning in the battle for my heart?

I decided, through the leadership of the Holy Spirit, to practically give God the opportunity to be that force of greater effect. I purposed in my heart to spend one hour every day praying and seeking God's transformation of my heart in this area. And with much rearranging of my life's priorities, I carved out an hour when I knew I could stay awake and focused and let the Lord minister to me. If meditation (prolonged thinking) on things of the world and devil had corrupted my heart, it was time for God to show His Word to be true and transform my heart in purity by meditating, as Philippians says, on pure things. What happened was one of the most life-changing weeks of my life.

I would sit and pray, not confessing sins or worrying about issues of the day, but primarily focusing on God. (If there are sins, certainly repent and confess them first - but the point is to focus on what God is doing in the moment, not what we've done in the past). I'd ask Him what His heart was toward me. I'd ask Him what He was working INTO my heart. I'd ask what He was working OUT of my heart. I'd ask Him to lead my thoughts and protect me from the thoughts of the enemy. Then I would just wait. I'd wait for thoughts that bore Spiritual fruit. I'd wait for revelation. I'd see what I started thinking about. What I discovered was shocking.

Night after night, I would start to think about things that I couldn't have conjured up if I had tried. God would speak to me about my identity in Him. He'd speak affirming words of love. He'd bring to mind things that I hadn't thought about in years but that were still wounds I subconsciously carried that affected my present more than I realized. Night after night, line upon line, revelation upon revelation, God would move in my thoughts and emotions to reveal things that He wanted to heal. It only took about a week before two things happened. One, I was profoundly changed and noticed a great measure of freedom that I had never previously walked in regarding this sin. Two, I was becoming another kind of addict: a prayer addict! I loved what God was doing so much that I began to long for free time to spend in prayer with God.

Don't think, "That can never be me. I can never love to pray like that." I have to confess that before this point, prayer was more of a chore that I was never really excited about. As I started to have faith that God would really do something in prayer and honor His Word, I approached it with expectation. This is when I started to see God really move. God's Word says that faith pleases God and we must come to Him with the expectation that He will meet us and reward us (Heb. 11:6). God will typically meet you in prayer to the degree that you expect Him to do so. The way we FEEL about doing Godly things reveals heart wounds. Just as we read in the MMM that it was shocking that God wanted to be exciting to me, I had to force myself to declare that God, prayer and obedience are exciting many times before I started to believe it. Our declarations and beliefs become our realities.

Let me be also be clear that the amount of time spent praying daily isn't the issue either; I'm not setting some formulaic prayer mandate out there that you can only be free if you pray an hour every day. This isn't about punching a prayer clock. But consider this: how much time do you and have you thrown away fueling lustful addictions? Lust based activity isn't a drag for you because it fills a wound in the soul - or at least attempts to. How much more satisfying do you think time with God can be as it truly fills that void and when we really start to see God at work? You may not have an hour - but pray in accordance with your faith; and even right now choose to allow faith to take root in your heart - this is about stirring yourself up to believe that God really is big enough to do what His Word says He'll do. Think about it, if you really and truly believed that God actually answered prayers, how much more time would you spend praying?! We put money in the bank because we believe it will bear interest. God promises that you'll reap what you sow - and His dividends are better!

Do you believe? Make a decision to step out of the comfort boat and walk on water into deepening RELATIONSHIP with God. Make walking and talking with Him a lifestyle! This lifestyle of letting God work things in and work things out of my heart has continued to bear consistent fruit as I have made it a lifestyle. I love it. Don't get me wrong, I have my stale times in prayer where I feel like I have been talking to the ceiling. But even when prayer is stale, God's Word promises that we will reap what we sow. We don't always understand how God is working in our hearts... but we don't have to. The Bible says that the Kingdom is like a man who scatters seed on the ground, goes to sleep and even though he doesn't understand how, the seed sprouts and grows (Mr. 4:26,27). If you will make heart change a priority and a lifestyle, God can do the work even in your sleep!

Many people are looking for a 3-step program or a spiritual warfare checklist that will guarantee their victory and freedom from this sin. The heart and the issues various men face are so deep and vast that we could never list them all. But the real "secret" to freedom is really so, so simple... and yet far more difficult for many who are looking for the "checklist path to freedom." It is easy to want a solution that you can check off your to-do list and then go on with "life as usual" apart from having to commit to something like relationship with God on nothing more than raw faith that God is who He says He is and will do what He says He'll do. But friend, let me tell you something, you were bought at a price. You are God's possession and inheritance. He is jealous for you. He DESIGNED freedom, real freedom, to ONLY be able to be attained through relationship with Him.

It is by God's intelligent, purposeful design that you can't attain total freedom apart from deepening intimacy with Him. He has designed life to work this way for both YOUR sake and for HIS sake. His desire is to delight in you and to fellowship with you. His desire for your sake is that your life have purpose and a higher calling. A higher calling is greater than yourself - you can only attain it through His ongoing influence and empowerment. So guess what? The very same principles that He is requiring you to apply in your life to seek Him, receive His grace, knowledge and power to overcome sin and to change are the same principles that you must continue to apply to fulfill your destiny and life's goal. He designed abundant life to only be attainable through relationship with Him. Relationship = freedom. He wants to fill "all in all" in your heart - and if He is not part of your life, that can never happen. Therefore, if He is not your All, there will be other things that will inevitably fill His place. Count on it.

Do you want to taste real heart change and freedom? Do you want to experience the thrill of knowing that your life is on the path the Master planned from before time began? Do you want to experience the joy and purpose that can only be attained by walking in your calling and bearing fruit? All of these blessings come as an outflow of deepening relationship with Father God. This is the path of the mighty man - to be fully unmighty in our own strength and to rest our strength solely on

Christ, the one true mighty man. This is the only path to transformation that I know. There couldn't be enough books written to cover every type and area of heart change that every person could face - and to seek this change in a book apart from the One who knows and designed your heart would only deprive you of the great joy of this intimacy with Father God. This is the only way to heal your marriage. This is the only way to truly have all your needs met. This is the only way to have your heart grow.

So I put the challenge out there to you: will you gladly embrace a walk of deepening friendship and love with your Savior? Will you put Him and His Word to the test that what He says is actually true and what He says He will do will actually take place? Take time to truly consider what type of prayer-life and Christian walk is required for you to begin to see transformation. Commit this to God and ask Him to free up the time to make a lifestyle with "God-fellowship" possible.

MASCULINITY WOUNDS:

A Common Wound – The Masculinity Wound and the Orphan Heart:

As you spend time with God, He'll reveal many, many things that you never knew were there. But in our ministry we see one very deep, profound wound so frequently that it should be covered. There are many, many wounds that men carry, but so many of them can trace back to a form of "Masculinity Wound"

"When I was a child, I spoke as a child, I understood as a child, I thought as a child; but when I became a man, I put away childish things" (1 Corinthians 13:11). Growing up, when I would read this passage I would think, "WHEN did Paul become a man and undergo this transformation of thought? What stage of his life did he KNOW he became a man?" That passage filtered through the lens of my cultural

understanding presumed that the transition to manhood is a process or a journey. So I pondered, "at what point could Paul look at his life and say, 'I've arrived!'"? Not only did my cultural limitations create an obstacle in my understanding, but it also left my soul bereft of the experience of Paul's account - I was a man according to my age, but still waiting to FEEL like one. Indeed, if it is to be properly understood and experienced in our culture, this passage needs more support text as we are lacking a key developmental component in our translation into adulthood: a rite of passage. To the Jew of the time during which Paul wrote and even in modern times, the answer to the question of "when do you BECOME a man" is simple and requires no more thought or text than is given in that passage. Paul had a rite of passage that marked his coming of age. There was no doubt in his mind as to the exact date and time that he could look back and say, "On that day I became a man." This experience and mentality is something that we have virtually no context for in our culture and age.

Many cultures world-over celebrate a rite of passage for their youth which commemorates and celebrates the passage to adulthood. For modern Jews, the B'nai (Bar or Bat) Mitzvah is that event. Typically at age 12 for girls and 13 for boys, this event both marks and celebrates a certain "arrival point" into developmental life landmarks. Whereas these may change slightly from family to family, the following points are widely embraced on some level along with this coming of age.

Spiritual Identity:

As a Bar (son of the) Mitzvah (covenant), this rite confirms that the young adult belongs to God in His family. Jews take for granted that they are God's hand-picked, chosen children – whereas so many Christian men never fully come to terms with the fact that God hand-picked them. We consequently suffer from a lack of spiritual identity and belonging, an "orphan heart," if you will, that constantly questions, "Am I good enough? Am I valuable and acceptable to God? Will He cast me away after sinning so badly?" Though the Bible teaches that we are fully adopted sons and daughters... we live like orphans with no real, deep-rooted identity. Instead of living as though we are owners and heirs of His house and kingdom, we live as ones on the fringes of grace hoping for morsels of blessing, love and acceptance.

Moral Accountability and Responsibility:

Jewish youths at their coming of age are recognized as being responsible for their own actions, spiritually qualified to read from the Torah and otherwise recognized as being spiritually mature. This also carries the responsibility of doing social good. This rite of passage induces a feeling that says, "You are CAPABLE and VALUABLE - in all ways spiritually, personally and socially." Conversely, many in our culture struggle with "failure to launch" - a term psychologists use to describe a person who never really develops adult self-sufficiency and responsibility for their own life let alone the community and world around them.

Most men have never been spiritually inducted into manhood. We are never taught that we are spiritually responsible and expected to have spiritual strength... so we continue to "think as a child" without maturing to a place of ownership of our own destiny and calling to our families, spheres of influence and world at large. Studies have shown that if a group of people see a crime or a person in need, the likelihood of someone acting to help drastically decreases from when an individual witnesses the same event. It is easy to assume that someone else will take responsibility. This is the same mentality of our culture. We must come to realize that the world and the Kingdom is our responsibility. When the individual comes of age in a rite of passage, the person takes sober responsibility for the spiritual climate of their day and the generations to follow. Apart from this launching point, many of us sit on the sidelines of life, waiting for God or someone to "pass the torch" to us. In reality, we already have the torch... and the flame is going out.

Capable of adult thought:

A b'nai mitzvah Jewish adolescent is recognized as having adult thoughts and may be included in adult affairs and decisions, votes at the synagogue, etc. I remember seeing the transition in all my young relatives around this age. Suddenly after dinner, they had interest in remaining at the table and engaging in the "adult conversations." However, most of our relatives would have downplayed their adult decision making abilities at this young age rather than affirming this change and nurturing it. Youths in our culture are virtually never affirmed. There is no celebration from their elders of the fact that they recognize that they are maturing and capable of adult decisions.

Too often, kids become rebellious in their early teens because they are not being affirmed or given respect. They try to prove to themselves and others that they are "individuals"... which makes the parents MORE controlling/less affirming... which makes more rebellion and identity crisis... this carries over to adult life. Many adults are still influenced by point-proving, rebellion, glory-seeking and a myriad of other emotions that negatively impact their testimony, relationships and efficacy for the Kingdom. Many try to gain identity from what they do, hobbies they practice and accomplishments they've had because deep down they are still trying to prove their individuality, value, independence and GAIN the attention and respect that should have been BESTOWED upon them.

Ability to Marry:

To this day, a carryover from traditions predating the Bar/Bat Mitzvah ceremonies, Jews recognize a son or a daughter of the covenant as being of legal age to marry (despite the fact that they are 12 or 13 years of age). In our culture, there aren't any marriages actually happening at this age, however the developmental affirmation and implications are significant. This act recognizes the adolescents' developing sexuality and doesn't skirt around the fact that these children are having adult sexual thoughts and feelings. I.e.: it affirms their sexuality.

Apart from "rite of passage" cultures, most parents unfortunately try to ignore, avoid and eschew the FACT that their 12 and 13 year olds are sexually developing; thus leaving the child unaffirmed as a sexual being, a masculine man or feminine woman. So rather than celebrating this monumental life transition, this ignorance gives a clear message that their sexuality is something the parent is ashamed/embarrassed or unwilling to recognize. Consequently, sexuality becomes a "secret" very personal thing and sexual identity is confused as the adolescent wonders about their changing bodies and emotions thinking, "Am I normal? Am I desirable? Am I able to satisfy someone? Etc." In search for answers, they turn to other sources than family and God to understand this secret, shameful part of their identity development.

Thus, in the absence of healthy family sexual identity affirmation, most young adults have a sexual identity that develops "in the dark" as opposed to an identity whereby they can say, "I'm proud of my sexual self." If you aren't proud of your sexuality, how will you EVER bring that part of you into your relationship with God? If you think sexuality is a dark, shameful part of your identity, you'll try to leave it "outside" the Throne Room with God. If your parents don't want to talk about your sexuality and nurture it, you certainly won't think that God would want to do so.

Contrast this with Biblical-era marriage sexual culture. In Bible times, "kids" age 13 and 14 (historically sometimes as young as 10 or 11 years old) would be married. Then, while all the friends and family continued to party at the marriage celebration, the couple would go into a tent in the midst of everyone and consummate the marriage while all the relatives continued the celebration outside. When the consummation was complete, they would come out of the tent with a bloody towel called the token, to show off to everyone and present as a gift to the father of the bride to demonstrate and celebrate their purity. Virginity and sexuality in that culture was not kept in the dark. It was a point of celebration. The token was a trophy of purity.

Sexuality wasn't something that took God by surprise or that He tolerates at a distance out of necessity. It is part of His divine design. The very first thing He told Adam and Eve to do after creating them was to go, be fruitful and multiply. Thus He instituted the sexual union and communion as the first Holy Sacrament - something to be celebrated - just as we celebrate communion - beautiful and pure. When God created man in the Garden - male and female - sexual beings - He said, "It is VERY GOOD." Tell God something He already knows right now. Say to Him, "My sexuality is very good!" Have you ever really stopped to consider that your sexuality brings God joy? Have you ever pictured Him blessing and celebrating it? If not, this is part of the problem. Have you ever pictured God present in your intimate times in marriage, enjoying and celebrating the union of you and your spouse? Do you see how far our cultural understanding of sexuality is from the heart of God? Is it any wonder that this is one of the greatest areas of darkness and perversion in our culture?

Bring this part of your being into the light. Sex and sexuality is not to be swept under the rug to get dirty. How different would our culture be if we affirmed, embraced, celebrated and acknowledged the changes that take place in our budding youths? They would grow to cherish their sexuality and keep it in the light rather than get it dirty in the dark.

Biblical Adoption:

These B'nai Mitzvah traditions date back to the Biblical idea of adoption which is different than our modern idea of adoption. Biblical "Adoption" was the rite of passage signifying the giving of the family name to a natural son (not bringing an orphan into the family as we understand it). Children around the age of 13 or younger, generally who had been apprenticed in a trade, were adopted – given the family name. Often a signatory ring showing their authority to act in the family's name, do business and trade with the family's credit, was a symbol of this (just as we read in the story of the Prodigal Son in Luke when the father places his ring on the son's hand - this act signified that the son received true adoption when he returned home; a more significant inheritance than the money he had previously asked for: the father's ring signified that he inherited the family name - his identity. The tradition of Biblical Adoption has numerous other similarities to the modern B'nai Mitzvah traditions as we've just read. Adoption solidified a definitive time when a child assumed their family and adult identity.

How does all this relate to our thought process as men and MASCULINITY WOUNDS? We run to porn because we feel like we're missing something, but really something is missing from us. We are living without masculine affirmation and are in a constant state of searching for masculine archetypes to complete us. Because we have never had a rite of passage in our culture, we have a whole generation of men who think like children. There was never a turning point or a place of approval.

Think of our culture's "rights of passage." When we turn 18 we can go to strip clubs and buy pornography, smoke and buy tobacco, gamble and buy weapons. To this day, I recall the letdown of my 18th birthday. My best friend, who shared the same birthday and I went out, bought lottery tickets, registered to vote, and smoked a cheap cigar before school… then we sat back and said, "That's it huh?" These are our cultural stamps of approval on "Adult Behavior." Kids become "adults" in the eyes of our culture long after tradition tells us that formative adulthood has been forming. By the time of our 18th birthday, rebellion, sexual confusion and moral irresponsibility has already set in; and "adulthood" freedoms as stated only lead to more self-destructive abilities without any significance attached to them. We aren't taught true sexuality, masculinity, approval, responsibility, spiritual affirmation, etc. We get a cigar and more of a "Good luck, kid… Welcome to the cold, cruel world of adulthood." Thus we stagger into manhood wondering why we never FEEL like men. We repress our sexuality and masculinity wounds and then wonder why we never shake our addictions and ACT like men.

We can't live an external reality of manhood with a nonexistent internal reality of adopted adulthood. We can't live like men if we don't feel and think like men – rather we grasp for answers, false definitions and ways to assert our sexual manhood. Never having received a definitive moment of fatherly approval and identity, as a cultural whole, we are disconnected from our roots and strive to prove ourselves due to an underlying sense of disapproval. Sin only compounds our insecurities and we live like orphans in the Father's house. We have a profound spiritual inheritance but live like spiritual paupers.

"Behold what manner of love the Father has bestowed (lavished) on us, that we should be called children of God!" (1 Jo. 3:1). The devil wants you, like the Prodigal Son, to think that Father God could never accept you as son again. Even the older brother in that story had an orphaned heart - all the father had was his and he didn't feel like he had the freedom to throw a party whenever he wanted. He was living like a servant in his dad's house.

When you inherit something, you can SPEND it. When God sets you free of an orphan spirit, He restores your sexuality, your identity, your inheritance, divine fellowship and so much more. Adopted sons get to be about their Father's business, wear His authority and "write checks" of faith that draw on the Father's heavenly bank account.

For all the promises of God in Him are Yes, and in Him Amen, to the glory of God through us. Now He who establishes us with you in Christ and has anointed us is God, who also has sealed us and given us the Spirit in our hearts as a guarantee (of our inheritance (cf. Eph.1:13,14))" (2 Cor. 1:20-22).

WORKBOOK MATERIALS

1) *God's answer took me by surprise, "You need some excitement in your life."* - Mighty Man Manual, p. 166. Does the above quote surprise you? Why or why not?

_____

_____

_____

2) For many of us, pornography is an outlet for excitement and passion. What happens when this "excitement" is gone? List some things, hobbies and interests you have and feel passionate about that can fill the void of time and excitement that lust addictions have created.

_____

_____

_____

3) How can you practically work some of these things into your life to fill the void that an absence of pornography may make in both your free time and in regards to escape, excitement and passionate activity.

_____

_____

_____

4) What does it mean to you to read that God wants to be your "All in all?" (See MMM p. 168)

_____

_____

_____

5) Read the following passage and answer the question that follows:
People spend a lot of time treating symptoms instead of diseases. When we have a headache, it is easy to take an aspirin and forget about the headache. But when the headaches persist, we usually begin to look for the real cause and cure the problem at the root. We tend to do the same thing with spiritual diseases. When we see an alcoholic, we go to task to treat the alcoholism and overlook the reasons why that person has a predisposition to that addiction. - Mighty Man Manual, p. 178

How does the above statement relate to your struggles and what can you do to start to discover the roots of addiction in your own heart?

_____

_____

_____

_____

_____

_____

6) God wants to meet your needs! Jesus taught us to pray "Give us today our daily bread" (Mt. 6:11). "And my God shall supply ALL (emphasis added) your need according to His riches in glory by Christ Jesus." (Php 4:19). List any roots or needs that you may be aware of or that God is showing you that have given a predisposition to this sin as a counterfeit substitute. Write them down below.

_____

_____

_____

_____

_____

_____

7) Now look at your previous list. Repent for agreeing with the enemy's solution for your need (just because there is an unmet need doesn't give you a license to sin). Ask God to show you how you can get this need filled in constructive ways. How can you change your priorities and/or life to allow yourself the ability to get these needs properly met? Write your answers below and be ready to encourage your fellow group members with what God teaches you about your needs... who knows how many others struggle with the same issues.

_____
_____
_____
_____
_____
_____

8) Think about the additional teaching from this session. How can you make a lifestyle of deeper prayer and fellowship with God a reality in your life?

_____
_____
_____

9) Think about the section on adoption and masculinity wounds. Does any of that resonate with you and your experience? What masculinity wounds do you see in your own life after reading that and how are they affecting you?

_____
_____
_____

---

10) Take some time to pray and get God's affirmation in the areas of these masculinity wounds and also use the following exercise to help heal those wounds as well as expose and heal many other wounds.

EXERCISE: HEALING HEART WOUNDS

If something that happened to you in the past is still causing pain and influencing thought and decisions in the PRESENT, it isn't past yet – it is unresolved present reality! Any event or memory that still hurts when you think about it is an OPEN wound that has never fully healed and is unresolved in Christ.

When a physical wound heals, you may have memory of the fact that you once had a wound there, but if you touch the spot it doesn't hurt any longer. This is how it is supposed to be when Christ heals our emotions. This is true for issues that may cause us to be tied to our temptations but also every painful experience of life. Yes, Jesus is actually that powerful, that real, that good and more so.

Apply this principle to any areas that may be wounded in your heart by following this exercise. First ask God to show you or try to think of a painful memory or a time when you were hurt by someone and thinking about it still "stings" or brings up negative feelings (anger, shame, embarrassment, etc). If it still stings, this memory has further healing that Jesus alone can bring. Follow these steps and see if you don't experience a miraculous breakthrough.

Step 1:

If there are any other people involved you first need to forgive them. Hint: if you can't pray a blessing for someone, you haven't forgiven them! The Bible has more to say about unforgiveness stopping God's blessing for you than any other topic. Furthermore, the Bible says that with the measure we use, it will be measured back to us... even to the point that if we don't forgive others, we can't be forgiven of our sins (Mt. 7:2, Mt. 6:15, Mt. 18:35, etc). It doesn't matter how badly someone hurt you when you consider that YOUR sins crucified the savior of the world. So we must give grace as we have been given great grace. If this is difficult, ask God for the grace to (1) forgive them and (2) see the person and their actions from God's perspective. You will be amazed how freeing this first step can be for you if you are carrying around the baggage of unforgiveness.

Step 2:

Now think about how you reacted to the event that caused the pain. In response to this person or event, did you act sinfully in any way? Did you know that if someone rejects you and you feel or "receive" their rejection, it is because you agreed with a lie from the enemy that you are rejected. If you know 100% that God never rejects you, it doesn't really matter if someone else rejects you... their opinion doesn't matter. Did you make any spiritual agreements by receiving a lie about yourself? There is only one opinion of you that matters... and it isn't even your own! Any time we "receive" a feeling or emotion about us that doesn't line up with God's will, we have agreed with the enemy and should repent. So if you sinned or agreed with any attitudes about yourself, simply repent and say, "I repent for the sin of agreeing with the enemy and I reject that bad opinion. I now receive God's opinion of me as sole truth."

Step 3:

Now that you are clear in this matter, God has the space to work. Think about the memory. It will probably already sting less. But now ask

Jesus to speak to you in this memory. Ask Him to show you what He would have said to you if He were standing beside you when it happened. Ask Him to give you perspective why the devil had space to do this. Hold Him to His word that says He works ALL things for good. Ask Him to show you how He can or has worked what the devil purposed for evil into good. Think what you would have said to you if you could be whispering in your ear at the time. Meditate as long as you have to until God ACTUALLY starts to minister to you about this. Expect Him to actually show up and do what His word says He will do. If he reveals any space that the enemy has taken because of this, reject that spirit and tell it to leave in Jesus's name.

Step 4
Once you have His perspective, ask for restoration. Ask the Holy Spirit to restore your mind and emotions to the state before this happened. Picture Jesus stepping into the middle of this event and taking your place - that is exactly what He did on the cross! You don't have to carry this around any longer. Jesus took your burden. Receive His gift of spiritual substitution - you get to be pure and heap it all on Jesus. You are absolved from blame. You can go forward from this moment as though this never happened to you. You can forgive any other people involved because they didn't do it to you - they did it to Jesus - and on the cross He said, "Father, forgive them. They don't know what they are doing." Again, continue to meditate on this idea of restoration until God does it! He really will!

Step 5:
Now take a moment to marvel at the new you and thank Jesus for His finished work. I can't tell you the number of abuses and bad, shameful memories God has healed to the point that I can hardly remember what it was like when I was still damaged and wounded. I have memories of the things that happened. I remember the tears... but I almost have a

hard time believing that I felt that way at one point. God really heals that deeply.

Now make your miracle your message! Write down what God did and spoke to you during this time. There may be other men in your group who are deeply moved and are themselves set free by your testimony!

_____

_____

_____

_____

_____

_____

_____

_____

_____

_____

PRAYER

Finally, ask God to speak to you about any wounds which you may be using porn to mask the pain. Think about any masculinity wounds that God may have revealed as you read this session. List them and use the pattern above to prayerfully receive your healing.

_____

_____

_____

_____

_____

Take time with God every day this week. Ask Him what He is working INTO your heart and what He is working OUT. Write down the things He reveals and heals.

Week 7
Virtue

MIGHTY MAN MANUAL READING:

Chapter 24: Virtue

OPENING PRAYER:

Father, You are the potter I am Your clay. I give you my mind, heart and body to mold. Grant me the grace right now to hear only Your truth and to be transformed. In Jesus' name, amen.

GOING DEEPER:

ADDITIONAL TEACHING FOR DEEPER REFLECTION

Freedom and victory come from who you ARE... not what you DO. Read that again. Your freedom and victory has far less to do with what you do and far more to do with WHO YOU ARE than you can ever imagine. Virtue, is a formation of character that runs so deep that it defines who you are. When people speak of "virtues" (i.e.: "patience is a virtue"), they refer to character traits that can't be taught or undone - they must be IN you to be expressed through you. A person who IS impatient will soon grow sick and tired of trying to ACT patient; but a person who has patience as a virtue, will be patient because it is part of their character, their identity. A person in whom purity is a virtue will be able to act purely without growing weary of it.

We hear the word virtue often associated with the concept of "a virtuous woman" or a "woman's virtue." This speaks not of what she does, but it is a purity that comes from within. We must become the definition of man's virtue. We must become virtuous men whose character runs so deep that it affects everything we do and inspires other men to follow. We are sons of the King. Sons of a king are groomed to run a kingdom. That is who we are. What you do will always flow from who you are.

Sometimes men write to our ministry who have been walking in freedom for a long time and then they have a slip up. They wonder, "How do I get back up after walking in victory for so long?" The answer really is simple: remember who you are. You are a son of God. You are no more a sex addict if it has been one minute, one month or one year since a slip up. God has made you a son, an heir, a priest and much more according to His Word and His work. When that truth DEFINES you, shapes how you see yourself, forms the very fabric of the reality from which you live your life, there will be no space for the sin any longer.

God has purposed that we should progress from sacrificial obedience to true unity with Him. This progression follows three general stages of growth. When first hearing the commands of God, the immature believer feels like they are burdensome and believes themselves to be really sacrificing something for God when they obey. That is to say, we look at what we FEEL like we are "giving up" and say, "Look at me, God... I'm really slaying the big one for you here, aren't I." With our actions we may comply with what we know to be right but in our heart we are kicking and screaming. As we mature, we progress to obedient disciples. A disciple is sober minded about the fact that they are going to go through testing. They agree with God's Word and CHOOSE to be happy about obedience. This is when real transformation begins and ushers us into the third stage. As we learn His heart and His ways, we naturally begin to TRULY love to do all that His Word commands. We love Him and His ways - we become like Him through our agreement and through His transforming work in our hearts. So we go from being slaves to sin, to slaves of righteousness, to disciples (ones who must discipline themselves) to sons.

"No longer do I call you servants, for a servant does not know what his master is doing; but I have called you friends, for all things that I heard from My Father I have made known to you" (Jn. 15:15). Just as it happened for the disciples on the day when Jesus told them He no longer considered them servants but friends, just as Paul writes of the "coming of age" when a son is no longer as a servant but an heir (Gal. 4), the final quantum leap in your heart takes place when you truly go from being a "slave of righteousness" to a "son of righteousness." Throughout this book and series, you have learned how to press down and overcome your desires... but God's plan is for your desires to change altogether; to progress to true Father-son relationship: *"And what agreement has the temple of God with idols? For you are the temple of the living God. As God has said: 'I will dwell in them And walk among them. I will be their God, And they shall be My people.' Therefore 'Come out from among them And be separate, says the Lord. Do not touch what is unclean, And I will receive you. I will be a Father to you, And*

you shall be My sons and daughters, Says the Lord Almighty'" (2 Cor. 6:16-18).

You are on an incredible journey. The sessions of this workbook are designed to take you on a very purposeful progression. Step-by-step, God will unfold the following plan in your life: to fall solely on the grace of God and to learn that this battle isn't about you; this provides the ability to receive God's unconditional love and the confidence to run to God and begin to dream again - to fight for your life as a prize; living with this vision "puts you in the fight" and gives you something to fight for when the enemy's attacks come; fighting and spiritual warfare reveals the needs and wounds of the heart; as God heals the wounds of the heart, He heals them by showing you your true identity; your true identity reshapes your reality and gives you the ability to relate to God and enter into relationship with Him as He intended from before time; finally, this great love affair with your Divine Father Creator will be the life you have always dreamed of. Do you see God's masterful plan playing out in the pages of this book and unfolding in your heart as He writes the epistle of your life? This plan, though obfuscated to those entrenched in the enemy's lies, when it becomes clear is so profoundly beautiful and simple that it should thrill your heart with joy to know that you are in the middle of God's plan for your life. When this plan unfolds in your heart, freedom is certain.

Just as every minute in the sun tans your skin... just as the presence of God made the face of Moses so radiant that no one could look at him... likewise every minute you spend basking in His glorious light and in His presence is forming His virtue in you and convincing your soul that you are indeed a called, purposed son and heir. As you become transformed, it is impossible that the enemy will continue to have space in your heart.

In the scriptures, we read many times when the demon possessed would encounter Christ, they'd beg for mercy and say, "Son of man, what have we to do with you" or more accurately, "What have we IN COMMON with you?" The devil's attempts at temptation paled in comparison to the deep identity that Christ carries as the Holy Son of God. Some of the definitions of Holy are "separate," "altogether higher and distinct." When identity in Christ becomes an active reality to the point that we truly have the mind of Christ, the enemy will look for an entrance into your heart, but cry out, "Mighty man, servant and son of God... what have we in common with you?"

Foundations of Identity:

Your spiritual identity in Christ goes infinitely deeper - both chronologically and circumstantially - than your sin identity. Have you ever stopped to consider the magnitude of your predestination in Christ? It is staggering to consider the words Paul penned by the Spirit, *"He chose us in Him before the foundation of the world, that we should be holy and without blame before Him in love, having predestined us to adoption as sons by Jesus Christ to Himself, according to the good pleasure of His will,"* (Eph 1:4-5). *"For whom He foreknew, He also predestined to be conformed to the image of His Son, that He might be the firstborn among many brethren"* (Rom 8:29).

Nothing is accidental about you. God created you with marvelous wisdom before the foundation of the world. He had a plan for your restoration into the likeness of how He created you and a plan to bring you back into His family - your family from before you ever sinned. He predestined the ongoing process of transformation of your heart into the very likeness of Christ, our elder brother and Lord. Your calling, the very gifting and plan for your life was set by His knowledge before you ever *knew to know* that you had a purpose.

David loved to contemplate this. Multiple times in the Psalms he also wrote about the wonder that God knew him and his personality intimately before he was ever formed in the womb. We are fearfully and wonderfully made. When God created you, He didn't create you as a sinful being because that would be impossible for a sinless creator. He knew that we'd be in a fallen world, but this flesh we are clothed with and sins we have struggled with are no more the real you than the

123

clothes you put on this morning. One day we will put off this "tent" as Paul calls it.

The Bible also teaches that Christ was slain from the foundation of the world (Rev 13:8). So we also know that atonement for sin and the final destruction of every enemy of Christ was likewise finished before God even started the clock of linear time. Even in the Old Testament, Jeremiah speaks of these wonders: *"Before I formed you in the womb I knew you; Before you were born I sanctified you; I ordained you a prophet to the nations"* (Jer. 1:5). The Old Testament saints were redeemed by looking FORWARD to Christ knowing that the price had already been paid. Considering theses great mysteries, why do we fear when we sin? Nothing that we do AFTER the foundation of the world trumps the plans of God which were set in motion and perfected BEFORE the foundation of the world. Do you see how this diffuses the lie that creeps in after we sin that causes us to believe that WE are so sinful; that God can't accept us? That lie was settled before time began!
This is very, very good news.

We have been taught to think, "I'm just a sinner, saved by grace." This is only a part-truth that wrongly supposes that we STARTED as sinners and then got cleaned up. The full truth is that you started as a SON, were born into a world with sin, and then got RESTORED to sonship. Your identity has nothing in common with sin or the world because your identity didn't start in this world. Your beginnings are from **before** the foundation of the world; and if you want to become a world-changer in Christ, you need to really get a hold of this truth.

When we seek to connect with this identity and the virtues inherent to it that are reflections of the goodness of God that He designed to dwell in us, we gain unshakable confidence due to the fact that we are not trying to pin our identity on the moment of our conversion or something that happened in linear time. We are, rather, connecting with the very intent of the Creator; with the very goodness, value and sonship that we possessed in Christ as part of Hi s original plan for creation.

Many have heard the old cliché definition of justified - "just-as-if-I'd never sinned." This is the truth: we can look at ourselves just as if we had never sinned, skipping over everything contrary to our nature through God's redemptive plan. However, without understanding this phenomenon, the devil easily steals away our foundation. We wrongly tend to see ourselves as vagrants who wander into God's house and somehow get adopted, rather than as full sons and heirs. For, we falsely reason, if the *foundation* of our identity happened at a moment *in time*, as we are led to believe, then shouldn't it follow that other moments in time also weigh upon that foundation, because all things temporal can be shaken? But we do not have a temporal hope or a foundation that can be shaken. Rather, like the Prodigal son, we were *originally* full heirs, wandered from our design and are restored to full sonship once again. Glory to God who named us, knew us, formed us, formulated a plan for us, called us His own, knew that we'd blow it, prepared the sacrifice of Christ for us unto re-adoption and even now has no qualms about the fact that in eternity past you were His and for all eternity you shall be in your Father's house. Amen!

Therefore we have all manner of confidence that identity change is not only assured... it is our destiny in Christ.

Reshaping Identity-Shaping Events

One day while praying and meditating on my Heavenly identity I dozed off - not heavy sleep, but what I call "preeping" (half praying/half sleeping). I had a couple short dreams each time I nodded off. In the one dream I was sitting at one of those tiny elementary school desks. In another short dream I was trying to get the approval of some boys at school. I woke up and shook off the sleep and thought to God, "Those are strange dreams." (Every time I say those words I have pretty much come to assume revelation is about to follow.) Suddenly I had a strong memory of a boy in second grade who brought some adult magazines to school in his book bag. All the boys were clamoring to get a peek. There was a lot of lust, a lot of curiosity and a lot of peer pressure to join in... and I did. I became one of the curious, lust-seeking boys that day. Afterward, I remember it became common for the boys at school to be on the hunt for porn to bring to class as their "trophy" to show the other boys. My friends and I spent hours trying to get our hands on pornography. I became one who was pursuing porn with curiosity and fervor. I even remember the pride I'd feel showing off a trophy I'd find and the power that gave me over the other boys who desperately wanted to get a peek.

We refer to virtues as being good character traits, but the Holy Spirit was showing me that at that time I made a virtue-level, identity forming decision to be one of them, "of the world," to identify with that curiosity, to identify with pursuit of lust, to let it have power over me and not to be set apart. This identity of being all about seeking to fill that curiosity still played out over and over in my present adult life. The part of the story I hadn't shared is that before this prayer time, I had been struggling with some thoughts spawned out of curiosity. I wondered if I could find some pornography that was unique to the particular thoughts that had been tempting me. That curiosity and desperation to find the object of that curiosity had tripped me a thousand times before. What I didn't realize was that those demonic thoughts were just like that black schoolbag with the dirty magazines of my youth; and I was battling a lie that formed at a young age that said, "You just HAVE to get a peek of that." And I wondered to what extent, my decision-making process was crippled because of the choice and identity I had formed all those years ago?

Quickly I imagined myself back in that scene from more than twenty years ago. Only this time, I knew my true identity. I pictured Jesus by my side and I told those boys that I am Jon Snyder, a pure son of God. I broke my false formation of identity and traded-up for my real, eternal identity. The ironic thing: when I was done praying... I couldn't have been LESS tempted; whereas in the past, those thoughts would have haunted me for days. The enemy lost his foothold.

I quickly asked God to show me any other identities or self-views that I took as life-defining characteristics about myself and used similar prayer warfare. I'm not trying to establish any doctrines on this: commit this to God and let Him lead you in it. However, I believe this is a good practice for all of us. Many things shape our identity - how we see ourselves and how we want others to see us. Our identities and self-perceptions affect what we do, how we think and act.

These areas of pride and areas of shame can often shape how we see ourselves and even leave doors open in the soul for the enemy's attacks. For instance: how does a man who has taken pride in an identity or a reputation as a ladies' man, adjust to a Christ-centered identity after conversion? If he took pride and self-confidence in a completely demonic identity trait, that agreement tints the way he relates to women and demands expression even later in life. How does the boy who was molested and used as a sex object by others cope with the feelings of powerlessness associated with an identity of being a sex-object? What if that individual even liked illicit sex acts on some level? These identity-shaping events continue to affect the way we see reality and respond to the enemy's temptations in the present day. We must become aware of and break fellowship with every area that we have enjoyed a reputation or taken on a persona that isn't centered in Christ if we are to fully take on His identity.

"Who am I?" This question of identity is one that philosophers and pundits have pondered through the ages. This is a much bigger issue and has even greater realms of freedom for every believer even beyond things that form our sexual identities. There are countless things that every man, woman and child on the planet "attach" to themselves as markers of their identity, self-esteem, reputation and the way they want others to perceive them. If your friends were asked the question, "What are you all about?" What would they say? What would you say to that question? What would your answer have been 10 years ago?

What do you want people to know about when they meet you? Do you want them to know you are successful? Do you want them to know that you are spiritual? Athletic? A sports fan? There is nothing wrong with any of these things... unless we take our value from them; unless they shape the way people see us or the way we want people to see us. What happens if the person who wants others to know he is successful is no longer successful? Does it affect his self-esteem or leave a hole in the heart? You see, every identity that doesn't draw worth from the fact that we are a child of God; that we are His prize and that He enjoys everything about us is potentially idolatrous. Even seemingly good virtues can actually be satan trying to get us off track. Wanting to be seen as smart, spiritual, reliable, patient, etc. Even the "good" identities can be based in pride, change or be taken away leaving us with a hole in our heart and questioning who we are and what our life is all about in their absence.

Seek God and ask Him to show you any ways you define yourself that aren't founded on the Rock of Christ as a foundation. Godly virtues walk a beautiful balance of confidence and humility. We can be completely confident in who we are as fully adopted sons of God while at the same time powerfully aware of our spiritual poverty apart from Christ. We understand that grace qualifies us and empowers us; and apart from that grace we are utterly as hopeless and helpless as infants. We walk with the confidence of kings, wearing crowns of glory, but knowing that we will gladly throw them at the feet of Christ on that final day.

Therefore let us shake off every reputation, everything that should cause pride, everything that should shape our identity apart from being nothing more than sons of God. This will transform your life and heart. Take time with the Lord and ask Him to show you any false reputations and identities that you may be carrying around with you. It is time for you to gain your identity, your calling, your inheritance. If you have to take hours and declare your identity a hundred times, do it.

Claim God's scriptures over your life, heart and calling. Destroy the agreements now and forever.

Workbook Materials

Virtue - Going from head knowledge to deep experiential reality.

1) Think about the reading from the workbook. There are 3 stages of obedience listed with landmarks along the way in each stage: slave of righteousness (obeying but not happy about it), disciple (disciplining yourself and choosing to be happy about it), son of righteousness (truly glad to walk in God's ways and commands). Which stage do you see yourself at? Why?

_____

_____

_____

2) Think about the transitional progression described in this session's Going Deeper. Grace = Greater confidence in God's ability opens the channels for it to not be about you. This gives the foundation to access His love freely and run to God for His transformation. This gives you renewed hope and a vision for your life beyond the mundane. That vision forms what you are fighting for and is the foundation for spiritual warfare. Spiritual warfare opens your eyes to the real needs and wounds that this has been filling. As God heals these areas, it formulates who you are and solidifies your true identity = Godly virtue. This identity forms the foundation for receiving God's love on a deeper lever and transforms you into a radical lover.

Do you see growth in each area and yourself going through the transformations above? Write down landmarks or insights that help you see change and growth in each of these areas of your heart.

Grace:

_____

_____

Love:

_____

_____

Vision:

_____

_____

Spiritual Warfare & Thoughtlife:

_____

_____

Heart Change:

_____

_____

Virtue & Identity:

_____

_____

3) Think about ways you view yourself. If you had to describe yourself to someone, what would be some of the things you'd tell them?

_____

_____

_____

_____

4) How many of these attributes listed above are based on Biblical truths and eternal virtues and how many are temporal descriptors?

_____

_____

_____

5) Take some time to pray and ask God if there are any views you hold about yourself, now or in the past, that were ungodly, unprofitable, proud or act in opposition to your destiny and identity in Christ. List them below.

_____

_____

_____

6) Look at the list of things God says about you below. Make them declarations of your identity by reciting them out loud.
- "I am the Temple of God" - 1 Corinthians 3:16
- "I am a son of God" - Galatians 3:26
- "I am no longer a slave" - Galatians 4:7
- "I am light to the world" - Ephesians 5:8
- "I am complete in Christ" - Colossians 2:10
- "I am a son of the light, NOT a son of darkness" - 1 Th. 5:5
- "I am strong. I have overcome the wicked one." - 1 John 2:14

7) Now make this even more personal. Ask God to speak to you in prayer. Ask Him what he sees in you. Ask Him things that He loves about you. Ask Him to speak about your calling. Ask Him to speak about your identity as a son. Write what God puts on your heart. Let all these realities sink in and reshape how you see yourself. You are God's son and will never be a sex addict - it isn't in your nature.

_____

_____

_____

_____

These statements above need to become your realities for heart change to take root. Rehearse them many times per day. Thank God for them. When you are tempted, quote those scriptures and remind yourself that you are a good man; a son of God, etc. Reject any thought that is contrary to these beliefs. There is no shortcut to real, lasting, virtuous heart change. You must rehearse it and allow God to set these convictions deep in your heart.

8) Think about how you view yourself today vs. ways you used to think and self-beliefs you had when you started this course. How is your self-perception changed/changing?

_____

_____

_____

9) As heart change takes place, the reasons NOT to sin begin to become more appealing than the reasons TO sin. The old way of thinking loses its power over us. List some of the new reasons not to sin that are more exciting to you than sinning.

_____

_____

_____

_____

EXERCISE:

When you are tempted next, try using these statements that affirm your new virtue.
1) Tell yourself and the enemy that this issue is SETTLED. The old me was tempted. The new me isn't like that.
2) Who I truly am is happier without porn and lust
3) Who I truly am will be glad that I didn't give in.

4) Who I truly am likes life without the devil's gimmicks

5) Who I truly am is strong in Christ, able to resist the devil, a son of the light and is repulsed by the things that used to excite the old me

6) Who I truly am has too much to live for to blow it on something cheap and worthless

7) Who I truly am can shape his destiny in Christ

8) Lust and pornography CANNOT be part of my life. It is gone from my nature and is not an option that the new me is willing to entertain.

9) Who I truly am is NOT going to be a slave.

10) Who I truly am is HAPPY to heed the Word of God.

PRAYER

Sample prayer of repentance - think of the ways you have seen yourself and even taken pride in over the years that are not Godly.

Father forgive me for every false perception about myself, my abilities, lack of abilities, talents, lack of talents, good areas, bad areas, successes, failures and everything that makes me either feel false pride or false shame. I now exchange all my false identities for my real identity as your son in whom you are well pleased. Let every good trait and blessing You give to me glorify You alone. Let every negative trait be now removed from my life as I confess that I have the mind of Christ and share in His blessing. Amen!

Ask God to reveal any false identities, reputations or prideful ways that shape your actions, attitudes and the way you want others to see and relate to you. Repent for any of these specifically and allow the light of who you truly are in Christ to eradicate these false beliefs.

Week 8
The Real Love Life!

MIGHTY MAN MANUAL READING:

Chapter 25: Expanded final chapter from Workbook

OPENING PRAYER:

Father, You are the potter I am Your clay. I give you my mind, heart and body to mold. Grant me the grace right now to hear only Your truth and to be transformed. In Jesus' name, amen.

GOING DEEPER:
ADDITIONAL TEACHING FOR DEEPER REFLECTION

GOD'S LOVE AND LOVING GOD

This radical love affair with our Lord begins, not with a great quest or great personal sacrifice of love. Rather the opposite is true. We begin to enter into this great love affair when we are stripped of all of our illusions: notions that we are able to bring anything to the table; that we have any ability to merit God's love; even the illusion that we are actually capable of loving God in and of ourselves. **God's love begets love. We can really only love to the degree that we have learned to receive love.**

Most of us think that it is all on us to love God. This is impossible! You can't give what you don't have. Beyond reciprocating love that we have received, the only thing that we can do is give God our *desire* to love Him more. Our "love tank" has to have something in it in order for love to flow from us. The reality for most of us as we awaken to this love journey is that our love level is pretty low. Our low level of love is why we fail.

Think about something for a moment. What if you had a "free pass" to sin? If God said to you right now, "If you desire, you have My permission to sin today." Carte blanche - lie, cheat, steal, look at porn, have an affair, speed in your car, etc. A "FREE" day to do whatever you want, have access to whatever you heart desires and you can "get away" with anything... what would you do? Would you sin? Our response to this is the gauge of our love level. Would you run off and sin?

Even without this "free pass" to sin, when was the last time you broke fellowship with God and found yourself choosing to chase after sin instead of loving God? **Every opportunity to sin is also an opportunity to love God.** Every choice to sin is a choice to leave His presence and break fellowship in that moment. But it takes a revelation of love to consistently make the right choice to love God more than our sin. When we have this, we have something that we will be willing to guard with our lives, thoughts and actions. This is the reason that God warns us to abide in Him and to keep His commandments. In essence He is saying, "Let me love you. Stay with Me and let My love transform you into lovers." But we have all gone astray and must use that as a reality check that tells us how desperately we must have a transformation in love.

The Bible has so much to say about the correlation between obeying God's commands as the evidence of our love versus the love of sin:

John 14: 15 "If you love Me, keep My commandments.... 21 He who has My commandments and keeps them, it is he who loves Me. And he who loves Me will be loved by My Father, and I will love him and manifest Myself to him." ... 23 Jesus answered and said to him, "If anyone loves Me, he will keep My word; and My Father will love him, and We will come to him and make Our home with him. 24 He who does not love Me does not keep My words; and the word which you hear is not Mine but the Father's who sent Me."

1 John 5:3 "For this is the love of God, that we keep His commandments. And His commandments are not burdensome."

2 John 1:6 "This is love, that we walk according to His commandments. This is the commandment, that as you have heard from the beginning, you should walk in it."

De. 11:1 "Therefore you shall love the Lord your God, and keep His charge, His statutes, His judgments, and His commandments always.

Just try doing an Old Testament search on this topic as well. You'll find over 50 verses where God equates keeping His commandments with loving Him.

It is time to depose the old master, the love of self and the flesh. Matthew 6:24 says, *"No one can serve two masters; for either he will hate the one and love the other, or else he will be loyal to the one and despise the other. You cannot serve God and mammon."* Love and obedience versus lusts and sins are in direct opposition to each other. Simply put, we will serve the master we love the most. You can't pretend that God is your first love if you keep running to another master. This double mindedness would be the same as trying to convince yourself and your wife that you love her the most after you have had affair after affair.

Your actions reveal the true yearnings of your heart. You see, you can't love someone and hate to spend time with them or despise their character. I can't say, "I love my wife," if I don't really care for her personality... if I don't love the things she does... if I don't really agree with what she stands for. Similarly, you can't SAY you love God and hate His ways, His Word and what He stands for. You can't say you love God but not have the actions and faithfulness to back up your words. We can't say we love God and look at spending time with Him as a drag.

This is a wake-up call: if you say you love someone but don't enjoy and delight in their ways, character, principles and everything about them, you actually love YOUR PERCEPTION of them... not the person themselves. You can't say you love someone and not make spending time with them a top priority. It is this time with God that allows Him to transform us. Friends, we need our hearts transformed by His love for us until we become radical lovers of Him who first loved us. The only thing that He requires is our time and a willing heart that desires to be made into a lover.

God isn't looking for slaves. He isn't looking for sacrifice. He isn't looking for people who will serve in Church and go to Bible studies. He isn't looking for people who do good things or who don't do bad things. He is looking for lovers… and a lover will DO these things and godly things by nature because they will be a person truly after God's own heart. A lover of God loves His Word, His ways, His statutes, His laws and His precepts.

The person who still sees God's ways as burdensome and who still thinks that their sin is comforting, exciting, liberating or freeing in some way is deceived and is still in agreement with the lies of the enemy. In their head they may want to serve God… but in their heart, they still love their sin and love the ways of the devil more than God. You can tell yourself 1000 times (and probably have) that you won't go back to sin. But until your heart is transformed in love, this desire will just be mere words.

What has been going on in your heart the last couple of days/weeks? Are you yearning more for sin than you yearn for more of God? Is keeping God's commandments burdensome? If the answer to these questions is "yes," you still have some love that must be birthed in your heart to take on that full identity as a lover of God. We must all come to grips with the fact that, based on our sin choices, maybe we don't love God as much as we may have thought if someone had asked us a few weeks ago. The good news is that you are not alone. Fathers of the faith like Peter also faced this dilemma; and everything you have learned up to this point is the foundation for this transition from the slave to sin to a son who truly loves the high privilege of loving the Father with both word and deed.

'

PETER'S RESTORATION IN LOVE

Now we all know the story of Peter's denial of Christ. In fact, the Bible tells us that ALL the disciples were scattered when Christ was crucified (Mt. 26:31, Mr. 14:27). The disciples all believed their Messiah would establish an earthly rule and Kingdom in His first advent. When that didn't happen, their perceptions, illusions, hopes and dreams went crashing to the ground.

However, one disciple in the story stands out in terms of faithfulness. John, referred to often as the one who Jesus **loved** and the one who **loved** Jesus is identified as the only disciple at the cross along with Mary, Jesus' mother and Mary Magdalene (John 19:26). These few all loved Jesus in a way that took them further than zeal, further than compulsion, further than their shattered hopes and dreams would go.

Your commitment level can never exceed your love level. No matter how zealous you feel at any time about never looking at pornography or how convicted you are that it is wrong, those feelings are just that... feelings. And when you are facing strong temptations, eventually that type of resolve will falter just as it did for Peter. But when Christ restored him, we see that love was the issue that Jesus focused on.

> John 21: *So when they had eaten breakfast, Jesus said to Simon Peter, "Simon, son of Jonah, do you love Me more than these?" He said to Him, "Yes, Lord; You know that I love You." He said to him, "Feed My lambs." He said to him again a second time, "Simon, son of Jonah, do you love Me?" He said to Him, "Yes, Lord; You know that I love You." He said to him, "Tend My sheep." He said to him the third time, "Simon, son of Jonah, do you love Me?" Peter was grieved because He said to him the third time, "Do you love Me?" And he said to Him, "Lord, You know all things; You know that I love You." Jesus said to him, "Feed My sheep. "Most assuredly, I say to you, when you were younger, you girded yourself and walked where you wished; but when you are old, you will stretch out your hands, and another will gird you and carry you where you do not wish." This He spoke, signifying by what death he would glorify God. And when He had spoken this, He said to him, "Follow Me."*

Jesus asked, "Do you love me more than these?" When all the zeal was gone, the feelings were gone, when faith seemed like it wasn't working, when there was nothing more to gain in a life laid down for

Christ and the vision of a future in-Christ was fading, Peter went back to fishing and an easy place of provision and comfort. There aren't a lot of words to mince in the passage above. Jesus tells it like it is: if you really and truly love me, you won't be able to go wherever you wish. There is a sacrifice in following Christ and the only place we find the strength for it is when we are sold out for love. The sacrifice is easy when the love level exceeds the requirement.

In the Greek text for the passage above, there are 2 words being used in this passage for the English word "love:" agape (perfect self-sacrificial love) and a lesser love, philia (brotherly kindness and affection). Two times Jesus asks Peter, "do you agape love me (do you love me perfectly)?" Peter downgrades the love level and says, "I philia love you." Then the third time Jesus asks, "Do you philia love me?" This is when Peter's feelings were hurt. Jesus says in essence, "Forget perfect love, do you even love me with brotherly kindness and affection?" Ouch.

Can you hear Jesus asking that question to you? We say, "Yes Lord. I love you." But then we think about our wandering heart. The "burden of His commandments... the burden, really, of loving Him. Like Peter, most Christians have a shallow love of God that must go deeper. Our lives and sins will show our love level for the depths of love we truly possess. If you had asked Peter before he denied Christ if he "agape" loved Him, the answer would have doubtlessly been, "Yes... I'll die for you." Peter was, after all, the one to draw a sword against a whole Roman guard a few nights prior in the garden when they came for Christ. But the reality was that Peter was willing to die for his self-seeking PERCEPTIONS of God. Now, wallowing in the aftermath of denial with the stink of fish all over him, when he saw his shallow love, Jesus asks if he really loves Him and all he can do is scale back his love and come up broke without an answer when the Lord asks him a third time.

I believe that many of you reading this are also facing the same revelation. I also had to come to terms that Jon, in reality, didn't love God as much as Jon, in theory, thought he did. I said I loved God...

but His ways were burdensome and I committed spiritual adultery and turned my back on Him daily, choosing sin that destroys over the God who loves. If God's word is true and "He who has My commandments and keeps them, it is he who loves Me"... then I had to look at my life and question, "God do I even love You at all?"

I think we all have to get to this BREAKING point to reach the TRANSFORMATION point. We must realize the poverty of our love and our inability to love in order to experience the riches of His transformational love; for if God's love was based on our ability to give any love or obedience to Him, then His love would be works-based rather than unconditional. Works void faith; works make Christ's sacrifice of no effect; works cause us to fall from grace (Ro. 4:14, Ga. 5:2,4). **We NEED to be in the place where we understand our abject poverty of love and where we know that God loves us, not because we are lovely but because HE IS LOVE.** This is the ONLY place where we can start to receive true love and be transformed. If you now realize the truth, that your love for God is pathetic, then and only then are you EXACTLY where God wants you to be. Only then do you start to receive unconditional love, not based in anything you do or bring to the table. Only then do you begin to transcend worldly love and experience agape, divine love that can never be shaken. He is your Maker. He created everything in your personality that makes you who you are. He fell in love with you before you even existed.

I believe something transformational happened when Jesus asked if even that lesser love was present in Peter's heart: the mighty Peter was finally broken; yet the Lord of Love was blowing on the embers of love that really were there, stirring him up, making him evaluate what he really and honestly loved deep in the core of his being. Jesus fans the flame of love, telling Peter that one day he will go so far as to die for love – the ultimate sacrifice.

In that place of brokenness is where the Lord begins to blow on the embers of love and awaken your heart. The Lord is blowing on the embers of love in your own heart even now. Who are you? What do you love? What do you *really* love? Do you love His ways more than the ways of the world? Do you love the testimonies, the end results of what godly living does in people's lives more than the testimonies of sin? We look at our lives and question the depths of our love... but deep down He blows on those smoldering embers of love and we cry out, "Lord, I know there is a real part of me that loves You. Help my shallow love. Create in me a real, deep love!"

Deep down, YOU love God as much as Peter did. It wounded Peter's heart to question if he really loved the Lord at all. If your heart is wounded at the revelation of your weak love, that only proves that God has something to work with. Deep down, you DO love, because he who has been forgiven much loves much. You ARE a radical God-lover - you just don't know it fully yet. And so we see that even though we have been double minded, even though our actions show forth our shallow love, we come alive through the fact that we have received some of God's love; and that fact has deposited a seedling of love in our hearts that is real. And it is this real, burning ember of love within our hearts that cries out to love God with a deepeningly pure, unselfish love.

These embers of love can grow hot when brought near the flame of God's love for us. Love can also grow cold. The good news is that this principle can work against our sin as well. We train our hearts to love the things we meditate upon. If we meditate upon lusts, we grow to love them and depend upon them. But if we draw near to God and meditate upon Him, our love for sin will grow cold and our passion for God will grow.

You are made for God's love. He is your lover and you are the object of His unconditional love. He isn't even asking you to bring anything to the table. Quite the opposite. He needs you to know that He loves you at your worst. He just wants you to come to His table, broken and aware of your love poverty. There He will pour out love upon you. His love will fill you. His love will transform you. His love will give you true identity and purpose. Then you will be able to love Him - not with your own love - but simply with whatever capacity He just gave to you. As His love gets into your heart, you fall more in love with Him and have a little more love to give back to the God who put His love in your heart.

It is so preposterous really. It takes God to love God - He has to give us the capacity to even love Him. As we choose more fellowship and love over sin as this grace enables, we, in turn, receive more of that love which simply transforms us all the more into sons with a little more ability to reciprocate a morsel of the Father's love. It is so simple and yet so contrary to logic. God says, "Love me." We try through works-based love and fail; thus the law becomes a tutor showing our desperate need for grace and salvation as the Bible teaches. When we surrender our pride and abilities, then through grace we receive God's own ability and true change.

There are books galore and sermons even more on the things that we receive from God. You can hardly turn on any TV preacher these days and not walk away thinking that God has nothing better to do than fix your family, fix your finances and heal whatever you wish... and I'm so grateful when God does all these things! But that is only half of the story of our love affair with the Lord. We don't hear about HIS inheritance very often - the thing that He died for: our love.

I remember a story I heard of 2 young men in Moravian seminary. In class they discussed unreached places for the Gospel. One island was completely closed to foreigners and missionaries. The only form of "immigration" their culture would allow were slaves sold to the inhabitants. So these young men came to the conclusion that they had to sell themselves into slavery to reach these people. Their families begged and pleaded with them not to go, not to do it. When they finally boarded the boat, never to be seen again, the one man's father pleaded, "Help me understand why you'd sell yourself into slavery. Why are you doing this to yourself? Why are you doing this to us?" The reply was unforgettable, "So that our Lord may receive all His reward for His labor."

To one whose life is lived by and for love, sacrifice is not burdensome. It is liberating. In all the commands of God you can either get the Law or the Love. "Go into all the world and preach the good news" can either be done "because God says so" or because you are moved with His love and compassion. To restrain our flesh and obey can be done for many reasons, but the command will be burdensome if it isn't done by love (and I believe that without love, eventually the enemy will win, because the heart still agrees with him).

DODGING BULLETS

Living by love will change everything. When you see a woman flaunting her sexuality, you can love her with Christ's love and not lust for her. You can choose love over lust when the devil tries to blindside you with his little attacks. I really find so many spiritual parallels in the Matrix movie. In one scene, Neo asks Morpheus in disbelief, "What are you saying? That I can dodge bullets?" Morpheus responds knowingly, "When the time comes... you won't have to."

When Neo "dies" at the end he can finally see past the natural. He sees the "code" operating behind what he could only previously see with his eyes. In that moment, he became impervious to the natural order and started living "supernaturally." Neo is finally able to look past the surface and see what is operating underneath, giving it power. When we are attacked by lust, there comes a time when we must be able to look past the surface and recognize the love needs of our own heart; and also see the love wounds in the heart of others that are causing them to be used by the enemy.

We must learn to take time and ponder God's heart in all things so that by His transforming grace we may think and feel the same way He does about people and temptations. This transformation is not inaccessible or years away. It is ready for the man who will answer and meditate upon the question God sets forth: Do you really love Me and My ways?... stay with Me. Spend time with Me.

Jesus said the two greatest commandments are to love your Lord God with all your heart, soul and strength; and to love your neighbor as yourself (Mt. 22:37). Every commandment is satisfied in these two things. Living by love transformed Peter from an angry man in a garden with a sword to a mighty man who helped change the culture of the entire world. Living by love is the destiny of every mighty man. There is no purer passion or rawer motivator. Nobody has to put a filter on your computer when you are living by love. Nobody has to hold you accountable when you are living by love. Nobody has to convince you that you shouldn't look at porn or lust after people when you live by love. These things will come as second nature.

Love and keeping God's commandments are reciprocal when this is our virtue. We keep his commandments because we love Him and we love Him because we fully agree with His ways and commandments. In this place, true intimacy with God comes naturally because our heart is aligned with His. And when we are truly intimate with Him, our purpose, our calling and destiny become manifest and accessible along with the grace to perform it and fight for it. This is the true warrior's romance... the calling and life of the mighty man of God.

BIRTHING A MIGHTY MAN... A MAN AFTER GOD'S OWN HEART...

David, of course, is the person who God identified, not only as a mighty man of valor, but as the man who was the most after His own heart. It is astounding to think that God's esteem of David was so great that one of the names for Jesus, the omnipotent King of Kings, is the "Son of David." Next to Jesus, David was the ultimate mighty man... an uncompromising warrior and a passionate lover of God. As you read David's Psalms, one theme surfaces over and over: his pursuit of God.

He identified himself as a lover of God's laws, statutes, precepts, judgments and ways. He truly loved them. They weren't a burden to him. God and His ways were his love. Radical love produces radical obedience and radical lives.

On a fundamental level, it is so simple to love God - simply keep His commandments, flee sin and run to Him. We can love God with our actions; and this is actually exciting to think that when we choose God over sin, we are actually saying with our actions, "I love you, Daddy." David was the one who said, he would not offer anything to the Lord that cost him nothing (2 Sam. 24:24). Love costs. I remember when I used to cry out to not have any temptation. Now when I consider that I can actually show God love with my obedience, that I can choose time with God over time in sin, that I can listen to the voice of the Spirit over the voice of the enemy, I actually don't mind temptation so much because, through obedience, I can give Him a sacrifice of love that costs me something. I want to know that there has been real love birthed in my heart so that when Jesus asks me like He asked Peter, "Do you love me more than these?" I can say, "Yes." I want a radical love-level that would rather die to my flesh and carnal desires than spend another minute apart from love.

When you love to serve God because you truly love Him and agree in your heart that all His ways and statutes are good as well as good for you, then the "burden" of not sinning will be gone. David loved time in God's presence. He loved to meditate on His word, to meditate on who God was, he loved to think about the beauty of the Lord. As you simply position yourself before God and allow His Spirit to pour out God's love for you, sin becomes vile and you start to form agreements that dictate the truth of your new man in Christ. Ultimately, only God can transform a heart and only time with God will position you for this to take place. As you come to the end of this book, I pray that it marks the beginning of a life of deeper pursuit of God - to lay hold of His amazing love and life. There is no temptation, nothing that you have faced or ever will face that can withstand the power of the love of God.

God's love for you is what you need to fulfill your destiny and walk in freedom now and forever.

WORKBOOK MATERIALS

1) Read the following verses and answer the question that follows:
"He who has My commandments and keeps them, it is he who loves Me. And he who loves Me will be loved by My Father, and I will love him and manifest Myself to him."- John 14:21

"Therefore you shall love the Lord your God, and keep His charge, His statutes, His judgments, and His commandments always. - De. 11:1
"If you love Me, keep My commandments. - Jn. 14:15

These verses can seem like an obligation to obey if we look at them as something we have to work up to on our own. Have you ever considered the heart of God as a lover giving these commands and the fact that He is the one who enables us, through grace, to be able to love Him? How does this view change the tone of these scriptures for you?

_____

_____

_____

2) In the past, have you found keeping God's commands burdensome? Do you still feel like you are "missing out" when you are being tempted? Why or why not?

_____

_____

_____

3) Read the following verses and answer the question that follows:

"No longer do I call you servants, for a servant does not know what his master is doing; but I have called you friends, for all things that I heard from My Father I have made known to you. "You did not choose Me, but I chose you and appointed you that you should go and bear fruit, and that your fruit should remain, that whatever you ask the Father in My name He may give you. - Jn. 15:15

As we mature and transition from slaves of righteousness to disciples to sons and friends, many of these passages include promises of blessing and greater intimacy. Why do you suppose that God entrusts more to us as we mature?

_____

_____

_____

4) Think about all the motives that you have for walking in freedom from sin. We have read that these motives when not out of love can be selfish. List your selfish motives and then pray for God to purify them in love. Hint: most likely, the things you want are things God also wants for you in His love and plans for your life.

_____

_____

_____

5) Does loving God seem like a difficult - even impossible thing? Why or why not?

_____

_____

_____

6) How does knowing that God's love is unconditional, that He not only tolerates you but actually enjoys you, celebrates you and yearns for your fellowship change your attitude about spending time with Him?

DAILY EXERCISES

The real goal of this section is really to begin to create a lifestyle of love that is sustainable and satisfying.

A) Make time to spend with God daily. Spend time reading the Word, listening to teaching, worshipping, praying, meditating on God and His attributes, sayings, words, character, feelings about you, etc. You'll go through seasons when some of these have greater focus and impact for you than others. The important thing is simply that sowing to your relationship with God be your greatest priority. Even if you hit a dry season, God promises that you'll still grow and reap what you sow.

B) When tempted, use that as an opportunity for expressing your love for God. "Do you love me more than these?" Jesus said to Peter. We can say, "Lord, I love you more than this sin." Every opportunity for the flesh is an opportunity to grow in love, intimacy and in the Spirit.

PRAYERS

Prayer to Position Yourself to Receive God's Love:

Father, I haven't loved you the way you deserve to be loved or the way I want to love you. I desire that the first and greatest motivator in all areas of my life would be love for You. Please help me now to experience your love for me in new and greater ways. Create in me a heart that is full of Your love so that I can love You and others as You love. Amen.

Prayer Exercise: the Wedding Night

When you have some time alone to spend with God, consider the following. Imagine that right now your life ended and you find yourself standing before the throne of God. Just like the Bible calls us the Bride of Christ, now like a young person on their wedding night, it is time to offer yourself to God. You have no more chances to get it right. All you have to offer is all of you. What will you say to Him? How do you perceive that He will receive you? What do you imagine that He will say to you? What will you talk about? Will He be pleased with you?

Allowing this scenario to play out in your mind will expose areas of shame, insecurities and help to cultivate intimacy with God. You may learn some things about yourself that you never knew were there. Allow God to speak to your heart in every area. Ask God to show you the things He loves about you. Use this exercise and write the things that God does in your heart.

_____

_____

_____

_____

_____

_____

WE'D LOVE YOUR FEEDBACK!

It is our sincere hope and prayer that this book and course has been a blessing to you. Do you have any testimonials of what God has done and taught you through this course? Do you have any input how we may improve this course? We'd love to hear from you. Please email Mighty Man Ministries using info@mightymanmanual.com. May God bless you!